The Death of Urbanism

Transitions through five stages of grief

Marcus White
Nano Langenheim

Contents

Preface

Figure 1: 'Great Guitar Street in 3D! – perspective view', detailed 3D streetscape point-cloud of Nguyễn Thiện Thuật, Phường 2, Quận 3, Hồ Chí Minh, Vietnam, 2019. HCMC produces 1/100th the CO2 per capita of Atlanta (Kenworthy 2003).

In this book we examine key historical city design approaches and 'procedures', along with recent urban design paradigms and some of their pitfalls. We conclude with more optimistic suggestions for advancing design responses for more equitable, healthy, sustainable and beautiful future cities. We balance this serious urban design research with a little dry and slightly black humour to help us light the way as we work through some dark and challenging, but critical urban issues.

The book is written for students and practitioners in architecture and urban design and related disciplines, as well as academics and non-academics with a keen interest in the built environment and the future of cities.

We would like to acknowledge the help of Tianyi Yang for her tireless contributions to image sourcing and production; Professor Mark Burry for his ongoing encouragement; Francis and Aster, for their sympathetic understanding whilst enduring 'half-parenting' for the past few months, who instead of acting out, put their energies into reading, practicing complex origami and creating truly spectacular craft projects, and finally, the AARD Curatorial Editor, Professor Rochus Urban Hinkel, who has been incredibly supportive of the authors.

Both authors have recently experienced the death of close family members. We have ourselves both gone through the various stages of grief. We have found the researching and writing of this book therapeutic and have both come to understand the importance of maintaining both hope and humour through difficult times – be they due to the loss of a loved one, the declining quality of the built environment, or the fears associated with bringing children into a pretty scary world where our politicians march towards the far right, and after decades of corruption, greed, and complacent inaction, climate change now threatens their future.

We would like to dedicate this book to the recently departed:

Mary Burke

and

Peter White

On death and dying urbanism

Back in black

Why do architects wear black? Is it because they are trying to disguise sedentary lifestyles, where black is used for its slimming properties just as they would use black to 'paint out' elements of buildings they wish were slimmer or weren't there? Probably not. Though most architects may have 'AutoCAD arms', they do seem to come in all shapes and sizes, including those who are as slender as Sejima columns.

Is it because of the architect's inner bogan*? Are architects secretly fans of heavy metal, the musical movement synonymous with wearing black, but due to a desire to maintain a professional appearance, are unable to proudly sport their favourite black band t-shirts? This may be true for some, (including the authors of this book) but the abysmal sales of our 'Architecture – not just for wankers' T-Shirt series would suggest otherwise [Figure 2 and Figure 3].

Is it because architects are all-powerful 'urban puppeteers' looming behind the scenes controlling the built environment and dictating people's lives? Hardly. Quantity surveyors and traffic engineers now have far more control over shaping the built

---

* *'Bogan' is Australian and New Zealand slang term for describing a person whose speech, behaviour and appearance are considered uncouth or unsophisticated, often dedicated fans of 1980s heavy metal bands such as Mötley Crüe or AC/DC who epitomise the 'boganesque'.*

environment than any architect. If anything, the black clothing is more likely to represent mourning over a complete loss of control over the urban environment and the decline of cities. In Rem Koolhaas's book with Bruce Mau, *S, M, L, XL,* he pronounced that *"urbanism is dead"* (1995) and that the uncontrollable generic city has taken over.

> *[...] The role of the architect in this phenomenon (manipulation of the urban landscape) is almost negligible. The only thing architects can do from time to time is to create within those circumstances, more or less masterful buildings (Koolhaas & Mau, 1995).*

Koolhaas describes the unfettered development within cities throughout the world with low-quality buildings designed in generic, non-descript architectural styles, built with little thought given to overall urban cohesion, connections, place, composition or much of anything other than to respond to market forces.

Cities are becoming or already have become manifestations of globalisation and 'genericness' like shopping malls or airports. In almost every international airport, one can either stare out onto the desolate expanse of tarmac covered in fossil fuel-guzzling vehicles, just like the endlessly sprawling

Figure 2: 'ArchitectyA : None More Black' from the 'Architecture – not just for wankers' T-Shirt series shows what architects are wearing on the inside, a modified Metallica t-shirt from the 'Black Album' (1991) replacing Hetfield, Ulrich, Hammett and Newsted with Hadid, Gehry, Koolhaas and Nouvel. www.zazzle.com.au/architectya

car-dominated landscapes of the suburbs, or wade through the anonymous no-placeness of the airport shopping mall with its H&M, Zara, and Gap, Duty-free perfume, cigarettes and liquor stores, Starbucks and Gloria Jean's coffee shops, Subway and

Figure 3: 'ArchitectyA : Plaster of Muppets' from the 'Architecture – not just for wankers' T-Shirt series, a modified Metallica from the 'Master of Puppets' album (1986) replacing field of military cross headstones with Le Corbusier's 1964 Ville Radieuse cruciform towers (note master of puppets pulling strings replaced with collaged hands from the famous photo of Le Corbusier pointing to the physical model of said scheme).

McDonalds fast-food restaurants. If not paying attention to subtle differences, it is difficult to discern where you are in the world. If not for the receipt from the over-priced burger you just ordered saying AUD and that the Burger King logo subtly swapped out for Hungry Jacks†, it would be very easy to believe

† The Burger King business name was already trademarked by a takeaway food shop in Adelaide when the franchise was first being established in Australia and was consequently renamed Hungry Jacks.

yourself to be anywhere, Mexico, Brazil, Hong Kong, Germany or North America.

Even older cities, once beyond the tightly controlled 'historic quarter' or old 'down-town' inner area, begin to blur into one another, with a scaled-up version of the airport's retail, topped with monotonous curtain walled commercial office towers or tightly packed housing towers with façade articulated by balconies sized to fit split system air conditioner condenser units.

As you travel beyond the central business district, the denser urban form fades towards lower density, single-use zoned suburbia. Again, the repetitive urban fabric is almost indistinguishable to the non-discerning eye – are you in Altadena on the outskirts of Los Angeles? Are you in Rueil-Malmaison on the edge of Paris? Or Tarneit in Melbourne's outer west? If you have ever travelled to Tarneit, it can be hard to not at least question the health of urbanism. For those readers who are not familiar with the term urbanism, it is both an abstract and concrete noun used to describe the conceptual and physical characteristics of a town or city. It is derived from urban which in turn comes from the Latin origin *urbanus*, from urbs 'city'. Ildefons Cerdà coined the term urbanism in his 1867 manifesto *Teoría General de la Urbanización* [General Theory of Urbanization] (Rippon, 2005) referring to the focus of the work done by an urban designer, who in terms of scale, works somewhere between that of a regional planner and that of an architect.

In 1859 Ildefons Cerdà produced plans for the extension 'Eixample' to Barcelona. Cerdà proscribed building heights, a carefully considered spatial structure and urban character with a direct relationship between streets and buildings, delicately balanced pedestrian and vehicular movement systems with in-ground and above ground services, and rigorous rules to ensure the protection of urban amenities such as light and air.

We will come back to Cerdà later, but for now, it is worth contemplating the level of careful consideration employed by Cerdà in the 1800s in contrast to the kind of globalised urban chaos described by Koolhaas or the monotonous, treeless, sidewalkless urban wasteland of Tarneit in Melbourne.

Urban decomposition

The death of urbanism is manifested in the slow death of many cities that are occurring around the world. We can find apparent evidence of the death of cities if we take an anthropomorphic approach and compare the human body to the city – a popular analogy with architects from Vitruvius, da Vinci, through to Le Corbusier. The death of urbanism might be confirmed if we think about the posthumous human body decomposition. The decomposition of the human body occurs in three phases. Firstly, *autolysis* (self-digestion), which begins immediately after death and involves circulatory systems consisting of cardiovascular (heart), pulmonary (lungs), systemic (arteries, veins, and vessels). The human body begins to eat itself – membranes in cells rupture and release enzymes that begin eating the cells from the inside out. If urbanism is indeed dead, we might think about the way many cities' transport systems have ground to a halt. Despite having undergone numerous 'urban surgery' attempts to prolong the life of most major cities via procedures such as freeway bypasses (coronary bypass) and road widenings (stents), commute times in many cities have increased well beyond the 'inflection point' of a 45 minute commute time limit.

The next phase of decay is *bloat*. Leaked enzymes from the first phase produce gasses that de-densifies the corpse leading to the body to double in size. Clear examples of cities that are very much in the bloat phase of decomposition can be found in North America including Atlanta, Boston, St Louis, Orlando and Houston, and in Australia Brisbane, Sydney and Melbourne spring to mind.

Finally, active *decay and skeletonisation*, where the liquefied internal organs are released from the body as it begins skeletal decomposition. For examples of how this plays out in urban form, see post-industrial European cities such as Turin and Frankfurt, more extreme cases in the rust belt cities in North America such as Detroit or, even more extreme, Katamatite in Australia which has about as much life-blood flowing through it as Guillermo del Toro's portrayal of Karl Ruprecht Kroenen in the movie Hell Boy.

Good grief

Urban design and urbanism have struggled to come to terms with the aforementioned losses, while also struggling with a myriad of other perceived or impending losses including the loss of environmental stability, loss of affordable housing options, loss of design control or influence, and a loss of urban amenity.

In this book, we will explore various key urban design paradigms transitioning through a (mis)appropriation of Swiss-born psychiatrist, Kübler-Ross' 'five stages of grief' from her seminal book, On Death and Dying – What the dying have to teach doctors, nurses, clergy & their own families (1973). The book is based on her research with terminal patients, dealing with loss in the post-modern world. In her book, Kübler-Ross explores multiple different types of emotional state, complex and dynamic types of grief, and coping mechanisms of people with incurable conditions. She touches on patients grieving past losses of health, mobility and independence, past losses of family members who had died, whilst also looking at losses and worries for their families, as well as the future loss and fear of death. She also traverses various emotional responses from patient's families as they try to make sense of and cope with their imminent loss. Kübler-Ross' book tackles these complex and mixed elements of past, present and future losses and a multitude of players by formulating the well-known concept of 'five stages of grief'. In our book, we will use these five stages as a loosely fitting construct to traverse recent urban design paradigms and responses to the aforementioned urban losses.

Our analogy of applying the 'stages of grief' to urban design paradigms, is used in part as a narrative device, structuring our review of paradigms and design approaches, and partially as an attempt to give a new insight into the complex, pessimistic world of post-optimistic urban design.

The topic of urbanism cannot be tackled in a traditional 'pure research' manner, is not necessarily singular or elegant and needs to take on board many facets and juxtapose many seemingly ill-fitting ideas. Just as Kübler-Ross' stages were not supposed to represent a formulaic linear progression, as Ira Byock M.D points out in the 2013 anniversary edition preface, our five stages are not strictly chronological nor mutually exclusive. And we will not strictly adhere to the death metaphor and will at times foray into pseudoscience and philosophy, design technology analysis, and popular culture.

Of course, this is not the first book that uses the themes surrounding death and grief to explore cities. In the early 1960s Jane Jacobs, (or 'gentrification Jane' as she is known in many unaffordable inner-urban suburbs where historic neighbourhood preservation quickly translated into pricing out low-income populations), wrote The Death and Life of Great American Cities (1961), in which she critiques the planning and architecture of the 1950s leading to the 'death' of traditional North American cities. This book was highly influential throughout the 60s and 70s being treated with bible-like reverence and in some places, still haunts university syllabus presented as a contemporary theory even today. There are quite a few critical themes, including densification and land-use diversity in Jacob's book related to urban grief that we will be returning to throughout the latter chapters of this book.

The five stages of grief are: *'denial'; 'anger'; 'bargaining'; 'depression'* and *'acceptance'*. These five stages are used as chapter headings, under which we symptomatically categorise design paradigms into the particular stages of grief. We will discuss key concepts of urban 'loss' that inform each of these paradigms and the design approaches and procedures used by each.

On urbanism (that is not dead or dying)

Before we launch into the five stages of grief, we feel it is useful to give a little bit of historical context discussing key themes of 'healthy' urbanism – connectivity, aesthetics and urban liveability to help frame the different urban design paradigms. We will talk a little about the birth of urbanism and the relationship between a population's needs and human aspirations or 'desires', the urban design paradigms, and the methods and procedures used by architects, urban designers and policymakers.

> *The city is not the manifestation of some iron law [but rather] the result of changing human aspirations (Lynch, 1981).*

The connected city: pack-donkey versus the 2D grid

Pre-Renaissance cities are generally described as either having grown organically – 'the pack donkey's way' or having derived from a two-dimensional grid plan.

> *The pack-donkey meanders along, mediates a little in his scatter-brained and distracted fashion, he zigzags in order to avoid larger stones, or ease the climb, or gain a little*

shade; he takes the line of least resistance (Le Corbusier, 1929).

Le Corbusier's concept of civilised humans planning cities with a 2D orthogonal grid in contrast to the unplanned, pack-donkey-organic layout echoed the thoughts of the British historian, Francis Haverfield, whose paper 'Ancient Town Planning' (1913) suggested the orthogonally planned grid distinguished the civilised from the 'moral inconsistency' of the barbarian. He argued that Rome's greatest gift to Europe was the definitive form of the town's rectangular grid. According to Haverfield 'The savage, inconsistent in his moral life, is equally inconsistent, equally unable to "keep straight", in his house-building and his road-making'.

The Roman design approach of ordered, gridded street layouts (aspects of the design paradigm), expressed the Empire's urban desire to reflect their accomplishments as a civilisation, with the physical form of cities appearing ordered and therefore 'civilised'. Another urban desire that influenced the orthogonal grid approach relates to efficient movement and city defence. The grid was believed to be useful for military access for defence from attacks and protect the city from uprisings from within, to keep under watch a restless population for surveillance, control and even repression (Kostof, 1991).

The layout of the Roman grid was possible because of technological advancements in design procedures, the understanding of scaled drawings and implementation (set out tools) such as the 'road measurer' or *hodometer* conceived of by Vitruvius, and the *groma*‡ which allowed the setting out of straight lines and right angles for gridded streets found in military camps and Roman settlements.

After the fall of the Roman Empire, Europe reverted to the irregular, unplanned growth around the spiritual and physical focus of the Church reflecting the social milieu. Gridded cities appeared again in the new towns in France and England (around 1100 AD) due to another change in society's prominent urban desires - the rekindled need for protection, fortified communities designed to counter each other's ceaseless raids. The revived interest in the grid plan was continued into the Renaissance, particularly after the rediscovery of the work of Vitruvius. Designers adopted the grid to create a new paradigm in the treatment of public spaces and amenity while maintaining political and military prerequisites.

The 2D grid would continue to be used for colonial settlements throughout the world. With the rise of the commerce agenda, 2D grid plans became

---

‡ *A 'groma' or 'surveyor's cross' was a primitive surveying device that used vertical staffs with cross members hanging plumb bobs. The surveyor's assistant would walk ahead and move around until their staff lined up with the surveyor's plum bobs.*

speculative, used in part due to the ease in which real estate could be divided up and sold.

> *Each lot, being of uniform shape, became a unit, like a coin, capable of ready appraisal and exchange (Mumford, 1940).*

The 2D grid method of planning was adopted all over the world. It was sometimes applied over sites regardless of topography resulting in areas of street grid too steep for a car to drive up. Notable examples are San Francisco California (the home of the movie car chase)§ and Wellington, New Zealand which was designed in England using 2D site plans without topographical information by a designer who had never visited the site.

> *'A city made for speed is made for success' (Le Corbusier, 1929).*

The rational nature of the grid and illustration of universal reason and human equality was appreciated

---

§ For a prime example of a grid laid out indiscriminately over undulating topography, see Bullitt, the 1968 police thriller film starring Steve McQueen, directed by Peter Yates, distributed by Warner Bros, where a 390 CID V8 Ford Mustang and two 1968 V8 Dodge Chargers chase each other around the steep streets of San Francisco becoming airborne at intersections. This example exposes the mismatch of 19th C gridded street layout, steep terrain and the speed of the 20th Century car.

by the Modernists who adopted the grid but began to give some streets prominence over others (Taylor, 2001). The idea of street hierarchy was elaborated on by German Modernist architect and urban designer, Ludwig Hilberseimer (1927) who argued that the hierarchy of major (wide) roads and narrow (minor) roads would satisfy the urban desire for safer streets for children, whilst increasing the overall speed of circulation of vehicles. This system was adopted by the Modern masters – Lucio Costa with Oscar Niemeyer in their built city, the capital of Brazil, Brasilia, as well as Le Corbusier's Chandigarh in India. The grid also reflected the classical tendencies of Le Corbusier's town planning (Laurence, 1993). A mutated version of Hilberseimer's street hierarchy occurred through the 1960s almost putting an end to the grid with serpentine street layouts for residential subdivisions. This proliferation of the highway, feeder and cul-de-sac system will be discussed later in the book.

The pretty city: a new perspective on the city

Though the gridded city resurfaced in some areas in Europe during the medieval period, organic town growth continued in other areas. Towards the end of this period, advancements in the artistic representation technique by Giotto (Giotto Di Bondone), and Masaccio (Tommaso Cassai) began to have an effect on the representation of cities. 'Bird's eye view'

Figure 4: 'Eunuchus', an early 2D | 3D drawn representation of urban setting, (Ulm, 1486).

Figure 5: Lithograph reproduction of Marco Polo's departure from Venice on his journey to China (CEA+, 1344).

drawings of cities in a pseudo perspective (somewhere between 2D and 3D) allowed for an overview of cities (Rowland, 1966). Though there was some idea of depth, the buildings shown in these drawings were not proportional, complying with the gothic tradition of using scale to set up a hierarchy of importance of figures and themes, not depth [Figure 4 and Figure 5].

In the early 1400s, prominent architect of the Italian Renaissance, Filippo Brunelleschi demonstrated the geometrical method of perspective by using a

Figure 6: Sketch of Brunelleschi's verification of geometric perspective technique, by White, M. based on illustration by Jim Anderson in Il Duomo: Brunelleschi, a Man of Many Talents (Atkins, 2008).

painting of the baptistry with a hole in it, standing in front of the building facing away from it holding a mirror [Figure 6]. The understanding of perspective was later formalised by the author, artist, architect, poet, linguist, and philosopher, Leon Battista Alberti in Della Pittura, a document that explained the procedure. This is noteworthy for two reasons. Firstly this is a clear example of the advantage of an architect being directly involved in developing their own design and representation procedures, a concept that we pursue in later chapters, and secondly, the new technique would lead to a new understanding of cities as potentially an urban composition, in turn, influencing society's urban desires.

The new understanding of the perspective procedure led to the city being represented with more accuracy as a whole, which helped to affect the public's understanding and informed urban aspirations for the city. These new desires, in turn, affected the urban design paradigm.

> *In the second half of the 16th century, the urban setting became a collective concern... a large number of perspective city views in which a great deal of information was combined in a realistic rendering. For the first time the entire heritage of the European cities was precisely represented according to the tenets of Renaissance visual culture and given general circulation. The population became accustomed to the synthetic perception of parts of the urban organism and the relationship between the city and the geographical setting. Perspective, the tool used to create these images was subsequently and continuously employed for the rectification of urban settings. The new rectilinear avenues became more frequent and longer, and better emphasised the view of the vanishing point (Benevolo & Ipsen, 1993).*

This application of perspective as an urban design technique impacted city design through the Renais-

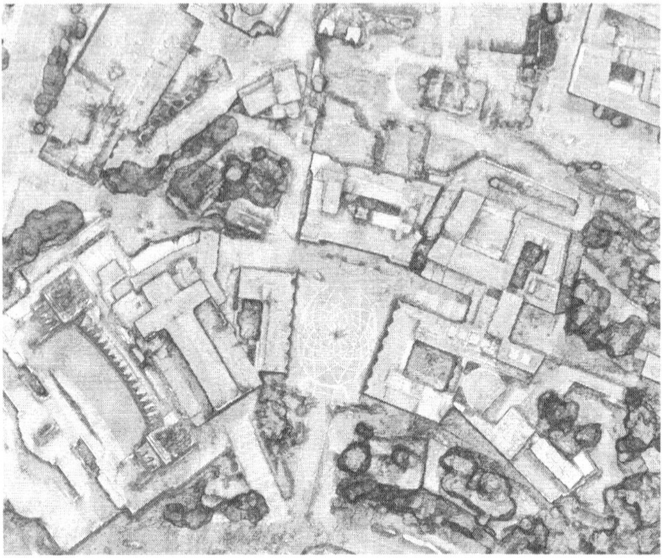

Figure 7: Photogrammetry point-cloud aerial view of the Michelangelo plan for the Capitoline Hill (Piazza del Campidoglio), map data: Google, Landsat/Copernicus.

sance and into the Baroque periods. During the 1400s the urban aspirations of the inhabitants of Rome varied from their predecessors. A new desire for an emphasis on the Church and the path of pilgrims was reflected with urban interventions – straight axial streets terminating in vistas marked by 'wayfinding' obelisks and religious buildings (Bacon, 1974). This urban design paradigm reflected the melding of the current urban aspirations and the new design technique – perspective.

A prime example of urban design paradigms taking into account a city's urban desires as well as expressing technological achievements (design procedures), is Michelangelo's Campidoglio (1546) which remodelled the Capitoline Hill to reflect Pope Paul III's vision for the new Rome, turning away from the Roman Forum towards the civic centre – St Peter's Basilica. The design involved 'tidying up' the space giving 'clarity and formal order' by adding a veneer of Renaissance façade creating a trapezoidal plaza space to achieve the desired perspectival effect [Figure 7 and Figure 8] (Mumford, 1940).

The potential of perspectival composition of urban form illustrated in the Campidoglio was explored further by French landscape architect to King Louis XIV of France, André Le Nôtre (1613 – 1700) who's design for the Palace of Versailles [Figure 9], emphasises axial composition and terminating

Figure 8: Photogrammetry point-cloud aerial view of the Capitoline Hill (Piazza del Campidoglio), map data: Google, Landsat|Copernicus.

Figure 9: Photogrammetry point-cloud aerial view of Louis XIV's Palace of Versailles (built 1668–74) gardens by André le Notre, map data: Google, Landsat/Copernicus.

vistas on a large scale. This bisecting axis created inspiring vistas that would influence many other designers internationally including Pierre L'Enfant in his design of Washington DC in 1791.

With the understanding of perspectival composition technique and the urban design paradigm came an understanding of the importance of the individual spectator's point of view, raising questions of whether urban composition was for the glory of God or the individual. The French philosopher and mathematician, René Descartes, a prime contributor to developing analytic geometry referred to as the Cartesian coordinate system (1637) suggested that space was the projection of thought where every viewpoint can be deduced, abstracted, from the universal position of a god for whom all viewpoints are instantaneously accessible. As noted by NYU academic Allen S. Weiss, depth is the function of ratiocination; depth exists because man is not God (1995). None the less, the importance of the individual human experience continued to be of interest. Weiss refers to the French philosopher, Merleau-Ponty:

> *...every perspectival projection... returns to the spectator's point of view, to that zero-degree visibility which is the pure latency of depth.... There is a fundamental "narcissism of vision" inherent in all systems of representation (1995).*

This 'narcissistic position' in perspectival representation seemed particularly evident in the picturesque movement of the 1700s. One of the aspirations (urban desires), of the wealthy English 'leisured class' was to show off their beautiful estates to colleagues during 'pleasure rides' (on horseback) [Figure 10]. English Landscape designers such as Capability Brown and Uvedale Price used the projected perspective views as a compositional tool, which in turn informed their landscape plans (Broglio, 2008). Key moments along a path were chosen as viewing points where one would dismount from the horse and view the perspective composition of the estate.

In most literal aesthetic observations, we might note that it is only in the "major" art of architecture and the "minor" art of gardening that the artist – and the spectator – may literally enter and explore the perspectival projection, taking his body into the very work of art (Weiss, 1995).

The picturesque design paradigm was possible because of the discovery and understanding of perspective, but it was also due to advancements in cartography and surveying. The concept of triangulation used for surveying being fully understood at a similar period. This triangulation would have allowed landscapers to sculpt the ground surface to gently roll under the sublime follies and artificial ruins.

Another example of urban scaled composition would occur over 50 years later in Paris, France between 1853 and 1869 with Baron von Haussmann's interventions into the Parisian urban fabric, which involved carving great boulevards through the medieval city, creating public squares and grand vistas to civic buildings. This major 'urban surgery' work recalled the perspectival interest of the Renaissance and the grandiose Baroque of Versailles.

The Austrian architect and city planning theoretician Camillo Sitte criticised the boulevards of Haussmann advocating curving or irregular streets for ever-changing vistas in lieu of 'a monotony of

Figure 10: Drawing of Warkworth Castle by Thomas Allom, Source: (Rose, Allom, & Pickering, 1835).

vistas, and an architectural ineffectiveness' (1986). Sitte argued that the city should be considered art, with a spatial and formal composition that preceded the considerable population explosion of his century. He suggested that the pre-industrial medieval cities had an inherent beauty forged by the intuitive creativity that shaped the irregular streets and public spaces. It would seem that the 'pack donkey' was better at urban composition than Haussmann or the modern planners thereafter.

Despite these critiques, the Baroque style boulevards of Haussmann would also be revisited on the other side of the Atlantic Ocean. In the 1890s and 1900s a reform movement known as *City Beautiful* recalled the planning of the Baroque mixed with

Beaux-Arts elements. The movement came to prominence in US cities such as Chicago and Washington D.C. which believed that the beautification of cities could counteract the moral decay of the poor, encouraging 'civic virtue' (Bluestone, 1988).

The concept of grand terminating vistas did not stop with the rise of Modernism. The capital of Brazil, Brasília, inaugurated in 1960, applied the CIAM¶ principles established in the Athens Charter of 1933. Designed by Brazilian urban designer Lúcio Costa with Oscar Niemeyer as the chief architect, Brasilia is essentially a gridded city bent in the centre, the *Eixo Monumental*. The focal point of this axis is the *Congresso Nacional*. Niemeyer and Costa worked closely to set up a strong relationship between the buildings and the city plan with the view down the centre of the axis used as the focus for perspectival composition. Similar to picturesque designers, the perspective image was used to drive the composition informing the plan. The composition of the towers, bowl and dome of the Congresso are enhanced by the planning of the avenue, and the editing of other less important buildings by either keeping them away from the Congresso buildings or by sink-

---

¶ *CIAM: Congrès International d'Architecture Moderne, (International Congress of Modern Architecture) founded in 1928, in Switzerland, group of Modernist architects led by Le Corbusier, Hélène de Mandrot, Sigfried Giedion with Hugo Häring, Pierre Jeanneret, Hannes Meyer and others.*

ing them into the ground [Figure 11 and Figure 12].

Suffice it to say, urban composition has been a critical element of urbanism over the past few centuries, in many cases literally shaping our cities. We will continue to return to this concept throughout the book, but will delve more deeply in the latter chapters.

The liveable, healthy city: urban amenity for humans

During the 19th Century, the industrial revolution brought the promise of better wages to cities, an alternative to the dire poverty of the countryside(Daunton, 2004). This new urban desire for workers to be located in close proximity to industry led to a great population increase and densification of cities. The cities were not well suited to these numbers and epidemics of diseases such as cholera and typhoid from polluted water, typhus spread by lice, 'summer diarrhoea' from flies feeding on horse manure and human waste contaminating food [Figure 13].

> *In 1851, a boy born in inner Liverpool had a life expectancy of only 26 years, compared with a boy born in the small market town of Okehampton, who could expect to live to 57 (Daunton, 2004).*

This dramatic difference in life expectancy was believed to be due to disease related to the foul odour coming from the human waste that covered the streets, as well as the tanneries which fill the neighbourhoods with the 'stench of animal putrefaction' (Sandlin, 2006). Surprisingly the common belief was that the problems were to do with 'bad air' due to a 'lack of through ventilation' of the cities as opposed to say, having people continually wading through excrement. The wish to improve airflow in cities became one of society's new prevailing urban desires.

> *...putrefaction and stench was also a threat to public health. Until the general acceptance of the germ theory of disease in the later 19th century, fevers and epidemics were explained by "miasmas", exhalations from decaying matter which poisoned the air (Daunton, 2004).*

John Snow**, the English physician-turned-anaesthetist, turned big data and geospatial analytics expert, is now considered to be one of the fathers of modern epidemiology. In 1850, Snow was a founding member of the Epidemiological Society of London formed in response to the cholera outbreaks of the time.

** *Not to be confused with Jon Snow 'The Pouting Bastard of Winterfell', short-lived 'King of the North' and the second most disappointing resolution of a character arc in GOT Season 8.*

Figure 11: Photogrammetry point-cloud aerial view down the Monumental Axis, map data: Google, Landsat|Copernicus.

Figure 12: Photogrammetry point-cloud aerial view of the less important administrative buildings 'edited' out of view of the Ministry of Justice building, map data: Google, Landsat|Copernicus, Image copyright 2019 Maxar Technologies.

Though these events were before the understanding of 'germ theory' and there was not an acceptance of the faecal-oral route of disease transmission, Snow was sceptical of the popular miasma theory. During a cholera outbreak in the mid-1850s, Snow rigorously sought out health records of recent deaths geo-referencing instances of cholera as well as in-ground service drinking water sources (point data) and produced a geospatial representation showing deaths from cholera in Soho London on Broad Street, Golden Square, and the surrounding neighbourhood, from 19th August, to the 30th of September 1854. A black mark was placed on the location of the houses where deaths occurred, as well as marking water pumps in the area. Snow estimated service areas for each pump – analysing walking distances and calculated areas that includes all properties within walking distance of each pump. By using catchment accessibility modelling (we are unsure if he used PedestrianCatch.com or ESRI's Network Analyst), he produced a kind of 'closest pump' Voronoi map to identify which pump citizens were most likely to use depending on their dwelling's location. These datasets were combined, and his map, along with statistical analyses, was used to identify patterns of clustering occurring around the Broad Street pump. It was later revealed that the well had been dug less than a meter away from an old cesspit which had begun to leak contaminated faecal bacteria

Figure 13: Engravings for 'Over London–by Rail from London: A Pilgrimage' by Stephane Pannemaker of a drawing by Paul Gustave Doré (1872), showing the overcrowded unsanitary conditions of London in the late 1800s.

from an earlier outbreak. It turns out that faecal matters††. Though met with considerable resistance from government officials – 'you know nothing John Snow' (Extra Credits, 2015), his compelling drawings, statistical graphs and argument for the connection between the water pump and cholera cases was sufficient to warrant the handle to be remove from the Broad Street pump, resulting in the happy ending of

†† *Sorry, that pun was irresistible.*

the rapid subsidence of the cholera epidemic in the area. In true progressive bureaucrat fashion, shortly after the outbreak had subsided, government officials replaced the pump handle. Fortunately, despite these efforts by the officials, the area was not subject to another outbreak.

Snow's combining of geospatial health and service data would go onto inform epidemiology, health planning research, urban analytics and informatics research, with influence spanning to this day. Incidentally, according to Michael Ramsay (2006), John Snow also administered chloroform to Queen Victoria on multiple occasions.

Let us now return to Baron von Haussmann's boulevards and their impact upon the concept of health and airflow in cities and the use of his 'subtractive' urban approach. Planning historians customarily attribute the origins of modern planning to Haussmann's plan for Paris commissioned by Napoleon III, between 1852 and 1870 (Neuman, 1998). In what Le Corbusier later described as 'urban surgery', Baron von Haussmann's renovation of Paris involved radical reshaping with the cutting of wide boulevards through the medieval city (Le Corbusier, 1929). The surgery was in direct response to the prevailing urban desire for improving the health crisis in a 'sick' Paris. The wide boulevards provided better airflow, created compositional terminating vistas, and at the same time accommodated a new modern sewerage system. It was Haussmann who objected to a proposal to channel human waste mixed with stormwater to flow into the Seine. Le Corbusier suggested that the boulevards 'were not based on strict deductions of the science of town planning. The measures he took were of a financial and military character', though Le Corbusier does go on to praise the urban surgery for having 'admirable foresight' opening the city up to the motorists or 'rabbits' as he describes them.

The *Haussmannisation* also involved strict rules for new buildings along the boulevards, with height limits and a set angle (45 degrees) applied to mansards for visual unity, but equally importantly, to ensure good daylight penetration (A. Jacobs, 1993). Haussmann's changes to Paris demonstrate a powerful cross over between the urban desires for health and military control.

At a similar time in Spain the Catalan urban planner Ildefons Cerdà, who we mentioned earlier, published his comprehensive theory of urbanisation, *Teoría General de la Urbanización,* with its five interconnected steps, covering theory, economics, law, administration and politics. As we touched on earlier, Cerdà was the first use the terms *urbanisation* and *urbanism*, both of which have become popular in the field of urban design.

Today everything is movement, everything is expansion, everything is communicativeness (Cerdà, 1867).

Prior to Cerdà publishing this study, Barcelona, much like Paris, had become extremely overcrowded and stricken with similar health problems and thus similar urban desires. In addition, the city had been closed to development beyond the medieval walls with real-estate prices unaffordable for the working class, so in addition to society's prevailing urban desire for the amenity of daylight and clean air, there was also a desire for affordability.

In 1859 Ildefons Cerdà produced plans for the extension 'Eixample' to Barcelona that embraced the grid layout with 45-degree chamfered corners and large diagonal avenues [Figure 14]. Unlike the urban desires for expressing civilisation or controlling a population, Cerdà believed the arrangement was to be an egalitarian, spatially just extension to the city. Cerdà's proposal was grounded in reality, seeking to adapt cities to the new needs for transport and expansion, by new, rail-based mobility, as well as the needs defined by the 'Hygienists'. Though Cerdà was aware of city remodelling that was happening elsewhere in Europe (such as Paxton's London, Haussmann's Paris and the Vienna Ring) his proposal to extend the city with a networked rail system was more holistic, than the interventions of Paxton

Figure 14: Noli map by Tianyi Yang showing the plan of Cerdà's Barcelona extension, map data: Mapbox and OSM.

and Haussmann. This was 'a new 'science of urbanization' for a complete city', one where 'buildings and the street were indivisible' where drainage, light sunshine and spatial quality was ensured (Rippon, 2005). Cerdà produced street sections that show a multitude of uses such as walking pedestrians, pedestrians dragging carts, horse-drawn carriages and light rail. 'He also designed the locations of services gas, telecommunications, and sewers' (Magrinyà & de Balanzó, 2015) [Figure 15].

Cerdà designed housing types around a perimeter block model, balancing bourgeoisie and working-class expectations with hygiene requirements

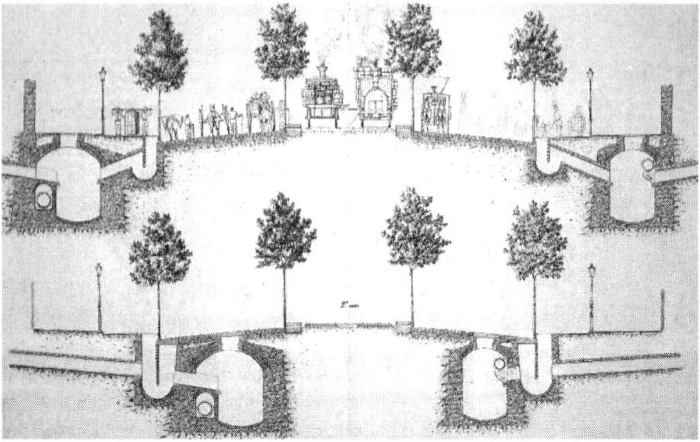

Figure 15: Street cross-section showing central rail network, horse and person-drawn cart lanes, pedestrian paths, stormwater drainage and sewerage, gas and water lines, light pole locations, with tree locations and sizes. Source: Museu d'Historia de la Ciutat, Barcelona (Cerdà, 1859).

and housing affordability. As one of the founders of modern urbanism, Cerdà is noteworthy not only because of his systematic analysis but because of his holistic multi-disciplinary approach to design.

Another influential urban designer concerned with urban health that came after Cerdà was Ebenezer Howard in the UK, who published *To-morrow: a Peaceful Path to Real Reform* in 1898 (reissued in 1902 as *Garden Cities of To-morrow*) in response to the 'great stink' and health problems of UK cities. What was needed was through-ventilation, the provision of parks to act as lungs for the cities, and 'a general process of cleansing' (Daunton, 2004).

Howard's Garden City zoned a mix of country and

city life, proposed a radial boulevard layout, central parks bounded by public buildings, encircled by the 'crystal palace', a kind of elongated glazed arcade shopping mall opening onto the park for shopping in 'most doubtful of weathers'. All this 'near to every dweller in the town', within '600 yards' [550 metres] from the furthest home. Moving out from the crystal palace was more discrete zoning, with a ring of schools and churches, with the industrial zone making up the outer ring surrounded by agriculture.

Unlike Cerdà's manifesto which was extraordinarily detailed and tested on the specific site of Barcelona as a 'case study', Howard's proposition was less resolved and included a disclaimer stating that the proposal was a 'diagram only' dependent on the eventually chosen site. This site unspecific aspect of Howard's proposal 'gave a new dimension to the town plan; a versatile freedom during its creation' (Lucey 1993).

Howard used the city of Adelaide, Australia as an example of how to deal with garden cities that grew beyond their capacity, by adding a satellite separated by parkland as is suggested by Colonel William Light's 1837 Adelaide plan (Howard was however mistaken, as both communities were laid out simultaneously) [Figure 16]. In 1903, English urban planner, Raymond Unwin put Howard's plans into practice with the town of Letchworth, the United Kingdom's first Garden City. Howard's plans were subsequently adopted around the world, seen as a new alternative to high-density cities, however much of the intent of the Garden City plan was over-looked or misinterpreted, resulting in new suburbs that did not have walkable access to civic buildings, parks, shopping or workplaces. His Crystal Palace mutated into what is now known as the shopping mall. Ironically, the idea of building on a green-field site was used to expand the cities of Britain devouring the countryside with the emphasis on low-density settlement being at least in part one of the major causes of 'suburban sprawl' (Laurence, 1993). We will come back to the concept of 'sprawl' in the next chapter.

Modern city planners also adopted the use of detailed city studies to make strategic recommendations to improve urban health and population movement. Scottish planner Patrick Geddes (1854-1932) is associated with the influential mantra of 'survey-analysis design' (SAD), an analogue precursor to Geodesign. The approach drew from the *scientific method* and involved conducting a detailed survey of a site, and through analysis of the data, the design would appear as a kind of scientifically determined outcome.

Geddes advocated 'diagnosis before treatment', considering the urban survey as indispensable to urban planning. Though there is still great support for engaging with site contexts, the approach has been criticised as too deterministic. University of

Figure 16: Noli plan by Tianyi Yang of The City of Adelaide, map data: Mapbox and OSM.

Greenwich academic, Tom Turner, suggests that the Geddes SAD method produced sad results. It should be 'put out to grass like a poor old tired horse' (Turner, 1991).

> *...the result of a pseudo-scientific, clean-hands, drawing-board-rooted design method. [...] One conducted a semi-scientific survey; one analysed the results (usually on drawings with jagged lines and arrows); then one performed a creative leap and produced a design. More often than not the design had little relationship to the survey and analysis. The method was not a success (Turner & Watson, 2000).*

Geddes' approach was more sensitive than Haussmann's or Le Corbusier's. Geddes preferred to engage in minor 'constructive and conservative surgery' making minor incisions in cities to improve the living conditions within poor quality housing, for example, widening narrow closes into the courtyard to enhance sunlight and airflow (Tyrwhitt, 1947). We will return to the wholistic diagnosis and treatment approach of Geddes towards the end of the book.

In contrast, to the more aggressive major amputations, bypass, or full organ transplants suggested by the 'urban surgeons' of the modern movement (see Haussmann's Paris or Le Corbusier's unrealised plans for Paris). They encouraged major renewal emphasising sterile repetition for efficiency and 'cleanliness', particularly in response to the post-war housing crisis. This architecture had a social conscience; it aimed to provide for all the inhabitants a social, an economic and above all, a democratic city, planned for all the people (Laurence1993). Their version of the scientific determinist urban design approach involved many testing speculative studies on the maximisation of housing capacity against minimisation of amenity loss. Gropius, Le Corbusier and Hilberseimer each used the design technique of physical models as well as drawn plans and sections with solar tables to work out their buildings effects on solar amenity – overshadowing [Figure 17].

The modernist urban design and architecture movement reflected a hopeful attitude in the face of adversity which was, as Kübler-Ross suggested, pervasive in other fields such as science and medicine:

> *And there were good reasons to be optimistic. Startling breakthroughs in physics, chemistry, engineering, and—to most people most important—medicine were occurring almost daily. Cures for hitherto lethal conditions such as pneumonia, sepsis, kidney failure, and severe trauma had become commonplace. Disease was increasingly seen as a problem to be*

solved. The sense was that medical science might soon be able to arrest aging and (subconsciously at least) possibly conquer death itself (Kübler-Ross, 1973).

This was the point at which many failures of modern planning were placed squarely upon modernist architects. Until this moment architects had been seen as infallible, able to solve all urban problems using modern architecture and urbanism, just as the best

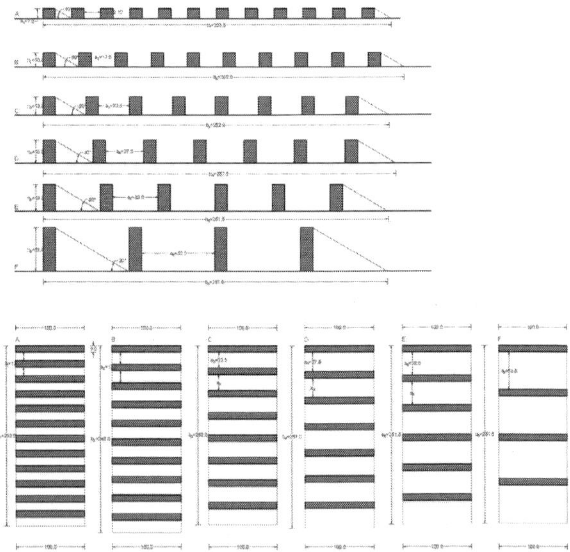

Figure 17: Walter Gropius solar analysis for a variety of urban form arrangements redrawn by Tianyi Yang.

physicians, during this same period, had been seen as those who could forestall death using modern medical treatments.

In this culture, the best doctors were the ones who could always find another treatment to forestall death. In the 1950s and 1960s, doctors rarely admitted when treatments weren't working and commonly failed to tell patients when further treatments would do more harm than good. Physician culture epitomized the never-say-die stance (Kübler-Ross, 1973).

But in 1973, the critical social eye that was turned on these extremely confident physicians and their procedural 'mistakes', was also turned on Modernist architects.The absolute trust of those pushing the modernist agenda had eroded. Individualistic genius architects like those epitomised by the Howard Roark character in Ayn Rand's 1943 classic novelThe Fountainhead were no longer to be trusted in quite the same way as they once were, as all-knowing visionaries at the top of the decision-making tree.

Almost at the same time that cities were investigating consolidated urban growth, the concept of high-density living was also being questioned. Modernist housing tower blocks that responded to mass housing shortages were being blamed for several social problems (Gallagher, 2001). The end of the long post-war boom heralded the start of two decades of intermittent recession and rising unemployment. New social problems would fester in Modernist housing schemes. In Britain, since the 1956 Housing Act, councils had been paying a premium for construction of blocks of flats. The apartments became filled with the current underclass and were beset with social problems and crime.

Le Corbusier's dream of concrete towers floating over lush landscapes was misread and reproduced *ad nauseam* without any of the pizzazz of his own built versions such as the Unité d'Habitation in Marseille, France. Instead of the green landscape rolling under the towers, the *pilotis* (columns) were filled in or became a landscape of car parking. A pivotal moment for these high-rise buildings occurred prior to 1973 in East London, when a structure known as Ronan Point partially collapsed due to a domestic natural gas explosion killing several occupants (Delatte Jr, 2009).

Contemporary atmosphere of loss

In the previous sections, we outlined three critical 'healthy urbanism' themes that occurred during historic moments within an atmosphere of optimism for an urban design future that was more connected, more beautiful, and healthier than what had come before.

The visionary example of Haussmann's Paris, and the holistic approach of Ildefons Cerdà in Barcelona demonstrate urbanism coming of age. These urban designers were grappling with balancing issues of movement by considering transportation and network connectivity. They were studying aesthetic unity and visual composition by designing for the human experience and composing from the human perspective. They were also responding to a desire for improving public health through their development of urban design procedures responding to desires for access to daylight, airflow, and sewerage in growing cities.

When we think about the atmosphere of contemporary society's urban concerns and wants, they appear somewhat more pessimistic than prior urban desires. The use of the grid expressed the 'civilised' nature of Roman society, perspectival urban compositions reflected cultural advancement, and the boulevards of Haussmann and chamfered grids of Cerdà were an expression of enlightened design defeating the disease and pestilence of the past. The focus of contemporary urban design is far less aspirational. We no longer talk about the future being better than it is now, we use terms like 'sustainability', that the best we can hope for is to sustain the lifestyle we currently have, and 'resilience', that we expect things are going to get horribly worse with a myriad of crises, and we hope that we can return to pre-crisis status quickly.

The driving force behind urban aspirations and desires now is based on perceived losses. The loss of cheap fuel due to peak oil; the loss of environmental stability due to climate change; the loss of time due to long commutes; the loss of social diversity due to planning regulation induced social segregation; the loss of health due to a worldwide obesity epidemic; as well as the continuing fear for a loss of amenity due to urbanisation and densification are all realities for which society needs to adjust and prepare.

In the following chapters, we will explore these loss-focused objectives and desires, as well as various responses to the suggested death of urbanism. We use the analogy of 'coping with loss', as the structure for our review of prevailing current and emerging urban design paradigms and their associated design techniques or 'procedures'. We use Kübler-Ross' concept of 'five stages of grief' from her book On Death and Dying, published in the pivotal year of 1973, with each chapter exploring a 'stage of grief' with its corresponding urban design paradigm.

In the First Stage: Denial chapter, we explore the coping mechanism of refusal to accept that the 'diagnosis' is correct, comparing terminal patient denial to advocates for business-as-usual urban 'sprawl' development, and some of the significant problems with this denial.

In the *Second Stage: Anger* chapter, we examine the placing of blame that can occur during difficult times of transition by examining anti-development community groups and attempt to tease out some of the underlying reasoning behind their anger.

In the *Third Stage: Bargaining* chapter, we move on to discuss the strong desire of terminal patients to want to go back to the way things were before they had been presented the bad news. We compare this yearning for the past with the revisionist New Urbanist design movement attempting to understand the embedded use of nostalgia and promises of 'clean' urban order.

In the *Fourth Stage: Depression* chapter, we study concepts of depression, starchitects, digital-procedural fetishism, and community co-design.

In the *Fifth Stage: Acceptance* chapter, we explore the idea of accepting our fate and making the most of the time left, presenting an optimistic manifesto that includes strategic densification, making speculative plans, proposing smarter community participation, and putting forward an integrated performance-based approach to urbanism.

First stage: Denial

‘this can’t really be happening’

Business as usual – continue to cul-de-sac(k) the city

The first stage of grief is *denial*. According to Kübler-Ross, denial is a healthy part of dealing with the uncomfortable and painful situation of their impending death. Denial functions as a buffer after unexpected, shocking news, allowing people to go on functioning as if nothing has changed. While they slowly come to terms with the shocking news, they go on with 'business as usual'. For the patients described by Kübler-Ross, denial allowed them to not face the truth that their way of life was coming to an end, a hard-fact that they were not ready to hear.

> *Among the over two hundred dying patients we have interviewed, most reacted to the awareness of a terminal illness at first with the statement, "No, not me, it cannot be true."*

> *One of our patients [...] was convinced that the X-rays were "mixed up"; she asked for reassurance that her pathology report could not possibly be back so soon and that another patient's report must have been marked with her name. When none of this could be confirmed, she quickly asked*

to leave the hospital, looking for another physician in the vain hope "to get a better explanation for my troubles." This patient went "shopping around" for many doctors, some of whom gave her reassuring answers, others of whom confirmed the previous suspicion. Whether confirmed or not, she reacted in the same manner; she asked for examination and re-examination, partially knowing that the original diagnosis was correct, but also seeking further evaluations in the hope that the first conclusion was indeed an error (Kübler-Ross, 1973).

As we mentioned in the previous chapter, architects, urban designers and associated urban professionals are anguishing over the death of urbanism while also experiencing poignant sorrow over a series of concurrent urban losses including the loss of environmental stability, biodiversity, urban health, social diversity and urban amenity. Many have responded in ways that closely resemble the denial stage described by Kübler-Ross. The response is 'this is not happening', 'these losses cannot be real', 'the diagnosis is incorrect'.

They then proceed with *business as usual* which involves continuing to facilitate 20th Century planning procedures of uncontained lateral urban expansion using low density, single-land-use zoning, car-dependent development pushing endlessly into cities' surrounding agricultural areas. The result of these planning procedures is sometimes called *urban sprawl*. As architectural historian Spiro Kostof pointed out, in sprawling development, residential areas are surrounded with moats of major roads and barricaded with noise walls with a single-entry road (1991). This form of suburbia is in a way a return to the walled medieval city, where the stone walls are replaced with concrete sound barriers, and the 'scatterbrained pack donkey's way' is reproduced by traffic engineers and town planners with asymmetrically planned streets and cul-de-sacs designed to slow traffic. Unfortunately, unlike the medieval fortress cities, markets and other civic buildings are not to be found within the suburban enclosure due to land-use zoning, a concept that we discuss later in this chapter.

In an ironic and somewhat tragic way, the symptoms of the losses the urban professionals are experiencing are worsened by many of the business as usual procedures they continue to apply in their state of denial. For those in denial, maintaining the current practice of suburban sprawl as though nothing is wrong, is like the patient with terminal lung cancer sitting in their wheelchair out the front of the hospital, just beyond the painted 'exclusion area', chain-smoking cigarettes. It is heartbreaking to see.

Climate change denial – denying the loss of environmental stability

To understand the urban design paradigm of denial, and the response of 'business as usual' we need to understand the current standard practice of lateral urban growth, and to understand lateral urban growth's link with the environment, energy use, CO_2 emissions and climate change.

The theory of climate change, which put simply, is that a build-up of greenhouse gases (predominantly CO_2) in the atmosphere traps the sun's heat, causing the earth's temperature to rise and altering the climate in different parts of the world. For a popular culture explanation of climate change, see 'Crimes of the Hot' Futurama (Avanzino, 2002). One of the major contributors of CO_2 and perhaps one of the apparent symbols of denial is the use of the car. In the US, 33% of CO_2 emissions come from cars and light trucks (US EPA, 2015). Australian sustainability researchers Peter Newman and Jeff Kenworthy have, over the past thirty years, documented evidence that increased density and improved public transport reduces 'car dependence', CO_2 emissions, and reliance on oil.

Density reduces transportation energy through several mechanisms: it shortens distances for all modes and makes of transit, bicycling, and walking more viable as alternatives to the car; it also reduces the number of journeys, since when transit is used, many journeys are combined –for example, shopping on the way to or from the train (P. G. Newman & Kenworthy, 1989).

US cities generate an average of 4,405 kg of CO_2 per person from passenger transport, whereas denser Western European cities generate lower at averaging 1,269 kilograms, and high-income Asian cities considerably lower at 825 kilograms (Kenworthy 2003). According to Mike Batty, Professor of Spatial Analysis and Planning at University College London, one of the critical problems with sprawl is 'environmental: low-density cities use more energy' (2003). This is supported by Stern, who states 'Spatial and strategic planning can affect patterns of energy consumption. Higher-density urban environments, for example, typically consume less energy for transport and in buildings' (2006).

Despite warnings by scientists such as Professor Peter Newton‡‡, the denial of climate change and the related need to change the urban fabric continues. Newton asserts, 'to maintain business as usual

---

‡‡ *Professor Peter Newton was a chief research scientist at CSIRO (Commonwealth Scientific and Industrial Research Organisation), the national government body for scientific research in Australia, and is now a research professor at Swinburne University's Centre for Urban Transitions.*

model of urban development is to condemn the future population and industry of that city to a sub-optimal living and working environment (1997). Denial is limiting the abilities of cities to evolve and shift to higher densities through transit-oriented developments (TOD) (P. Newman, 2014), to develop planning policies that accelerate the urban infrastructures' transformations necessary to provide inclusive, comfortable walking access to shops, healthy food, public transport, parks and recreation facilities. Given the direct relationship between the environment and urban form, it may be helpful to give a bit of a quick recap of the context of climate change and climate change denial discussion. As we unpack these concepts, it is worth remembering Kübler-Ross' stages are not necessarily a linear progression, with denial particularly seeming to occur in waves. This has been very much the case with the response to climate change.

Though a consensus began to form in the scientific community that anthropogenic carbon dioxide warming was occurring in the 1980s (Hansen et al., 1981), there was a sense of denial and warnings were ignored. But after the dogged efforts of scientific researchers and formation of the Intergovernmental Panel on Climate Change (IPCC) established in 1988 by the World Meteorological Organization (WMO) and the United Nations Environment Programme (UNEP), eventually, it seemed like there was a breakthrough.

Around ten years ago, there appeared to be a consensus amongst the populous, in most western countries at least, that climate change was real, and that immediate action was needed to avert impending environmental disaster. The documentary by Al Gore, *An Inconvenient Truth,* also increased the prominence of climate change in the media and political discussions around the world. Global warming was moved to the top of desire lists for many cities and counties. During his visit to Australia, Gore caused a media stir when he compared John Howard, then the Prime Minister of Australia, to those who believe the earth is flat, 'though there are some people who still think it's flat, we generally ignore that view because the evidence has mounted to the point where we understand that it shouldn't be taken seriously' (Gore, 2006).

In the UK in the same year, economist Nicholas Stern released the 'Stern Review on the Economics of Climate Change', a report for the British government. Stern argued that there needed to be a decisive investment in combating climate change immediately, failing to do so could have dramatic impacts on global finance with GDP being up to twenty per cent lower than it otherwise might be in some countries (Stern 2006).

There was strong momentum internationally with left-leaning governments seizing power who had campaigned with the platform of climate action through carbon pricing. In the US, President Obama established the White House Office of Energy and Climate Change Policy, and released the President's 21st Century Clean Transportation Plan intending to reduce carbon pollution.

In Australia, a clear sign of climate change moving into the mainstream political debate was a speech for the Annual Fraser Lecture at the Belconnen Labor Club in Canberra, 30th May 2007 from Kevin Rudd, then the leader of the federal opposition who stated:

> *Climate change is already a reality – an undeniable reality. You can see it in the drought – the worst in living memory. You can see it in our depleting water supplies and crippling water restrictions. You can see it in the Murray River running dry. You can see it in rising temperatures – 11 of the 12 warmest years on record occurred between 1995 and 2006. You can see it in the melting of the Arctic ice cap retreating mountain glaciers, and rising sea levels. The core science of climate change is not in dispute (Rudd 2007).*

After a landslide election victory later that year, Rudd's government put forward a Carbon Pollution Reduction Scheme (CPRS). The Rudd government proposed a super-profits mining tax. Acting quickly, the mining industry launched an aggressive attack campaign spending more than $20 million on an advertising campaign targeting the government's mining tax. The campaign was discontinued, when Kevin Rudd was removed as Labor leader and Prime Minister by his own caucus (Crabb, 2018).

Australia has played a strange kind of government and opposition party leader whack-a-mole since Rudd's removal. Prime Ministers have ranged from those who would do something if it wasn't so politically toxic, to the open deniers 'climate change is crap', to our current (at least at the time of writing this book) Prime Minister whose career highlight so far is when he brought a piece of coal into parliament to use as a prop in support of continuing to build new coal mines stating 'this is coal – don't be afraid, don't be scared'[§§].

Since the early 2000s, industry groups and right-wing think tanks have pushed back against the momentum that had been building around global action on climate change. Australia under the leadership of Prime Minister Morrison has continued alongside the US under the leadership of President Trump, (both amongst the highest per-capita polluting countries in the world) to remain in their state of denial. In 2017, President Trump signed an executive order aimed towards boosting the coal industry that rolls

---

§§ *Very much feeling the fourth stage whilst writing this paragraph.*

back on Obama-era climate regulations (Merica, 2017).

Denial and diagnosis-shopping

In the denial stage, it is common to for terminal patients to go 'diagnosis-shopping', where they seek out and interpret information that reinforces or proves their own belief that there must be some kind of mistake and that they are just fine. In Kübler-Ross's example of diagnosis-shopping, the patient went looking for another physician who would provide a more favourable finding requesting examination and re-examination. This diagnosis-shopping is even easier now with the use of 'Dr Google' where one can use the ubiquitous search engine to search symptoms and filter the results based on the answers you would like to hear. This kind of confirmation bias is also amplified by social media 'echo chambers' or what political activist Eli Pariser calls the 'filter bubbles' (2011), where your search history and web-site views influence your algorithm-based news feeds to further confirm their desirable-outcome medical hypothesis.

Like Kübler-Ross's example the patient's favourable diagnosis-shopping, urban planners and policymakers in the denial stage also shop for 'expert researcher' and data to support their position, whether it is that climate change is not real, that car-dependent sprawl is good, or that living on the urban fringe is affordable. It is easy to find confirmation of a view that the best cause of action is to continue with business-as-usual.

> *There is a narrow view that suggests that sprawl is no more or less than the efficient operation of the land market, and in this sense, is the outcome of a competitive process. The problem with this is that no process of development exists within a purely competitive market, indeed sprawl might be seen as the failure of the market to take account of the longer-term economic externalities in favour of 'short termism'. And of course, social and qualitative environmental issues are rarely considered in this kind of debate (Batty et al., 2003).*

The 'narrow view' mentioned here refers to those critics opposing consolidation policies such as Randal O'Tool, Wendell Cox and Joel Kotkin in the US, and in Australia Tony Recsei, Patrick Troy, Miles Lewis, Bob Birrell, and Kevin O'Connor – the Pro-Sprawl or 'Anti-anti-sprawl' advocates.

When one is diagnosis-shopping for confirmation that everything is fine, it is hard to go past Professor Robert Bruegmann (The University of Illinois at Chicago), known for his critical position on urban consolidation. Bruegmann suggests that suburbia is the expression of 'free markets' and is an outcome of 'our democracy' (Bruegmann, 2006). These are common themes in pro-sprawl rhetoric, appealing to the North American's desire to express 'freedom'. They see urban consolidation by use of growth boundaries and stipulated 'mixed-use' zoning as infringements on people's civil liberties, yet they seem quite happy to have single-use zoning, maximum height limits, and density restrictions enforced.

In a good example of diagnosis-shopping, Professor Robert Bruegmann was invited to Sydney, Australia to give a public lecture attended by members of the Save Our Suburbs (SOS) lobby group. Tony Recsei, the New South Wales SOS president at the time, said of Bruegmann that he:

> *...gave a masterly lecture in which he discussed the pros and cons of 'sprawl' versus 'consolidation'. His overheads made quite clear what we have been saying all along – the benefits claimed for "consolidation" do not happen... [state governments are] forcing high density onto unwilling communities under the threat of taking away the planning powers of their councils (Recsei, 2004).*

US economist Randal O'Toole, long-time critic of planning policies in Portland Oregon, suggests that low densities provide benefits that people value, including 'lower land costs, private yards with gardens and play areas, less congested roads, proximity to recreation areas, and access to a wide variety of low-cost consumer goods and services'. 'Few Americans are willing to give up their automobiles, single-family homes, and large backyards' (O'Toole 2001). Unlike almost all urban design critics since the early 1970s, O'Toole supports traffic-engineered freeway solutions like the freeway bypasses (coronary bypass) we mentioned earlier in the book. In a public lecture, O'Tool was reported saying:

> *...they're actually building roads in Houston... They know something in Houston that we haven't figured out here. You can build your way out of a traffic problem (Griffin, 2007).*

This is particularly interesting as Houston is often cited on lists of the world's worst cities, one of the most sprawling cities, one of the highest per capita polluters, and consistently ranks in the top five 'fattest cities' in the US (P. G. Newman & Kenworthy, 1989; Millado & Vigneri, 2012; Sui, 2003).

Another talking point that is prominent when one is confirmation-bias diagnosis-shopping, at least in the US, is that densification is just another liberal elite conspiracy. Here, the argument put forward is that the high-class professional population is trying to rob potential fringe dwellers of owning their own detached home, 'like the City Beautiful and Prohibition reform movements before it, the anti-sprawl movement has been heavily supported by individuals drawn from an upper-middle-class professional population... from an elite group of academics, central-city business leaders' (Bruegmann, 2006).

Denying the symptoms of sprawl in an ungainly way

The Compact Oxford English Dictionary defines the word *sprawl as* 'to sit, lie, or fall with one's limbs spread out in an ungainly way; (as adj.) sprawling spread out irregularly over a large area. In a document measuring the impacts of sprawl in the US, Reid Ewing defines 'sprawl' as:

> *... [having] four dimensions: a population that is widely dispersed in low-density development; rigidly separated homes, shops, and workplaces; a network of roads marked by huge blocks and poor access; and a lack of well-defined, thriving activity centres, such as downtowns and town centres. Most of the other features usually associated with sprawl — the lack of transportation choices, relative uniformity of housing options or the difficulty of*

walking — are a result of these conditions (R. H. Ewing, Pendall, & Chen, 2002).

Failure of Euclidian zoning - denying the loss of land-use-mix

How a population is distributed within a city has been and remains a crucial factor of urbanism. Though the technique of land-use zoning had been adopted in many cities in Europe, and to a lesser extent in some cities in the US, New York City's zoning ordinances in 1916 are commonly considered to be the first modern use of zoning. What began as a procedure for land-use separation became the premise for a whole urban design paradigm.

Driven by a desire to separate lower class fabric markets from the upscale retailers of 5th Avenue, as well as reducing density for the health, safety, and wellbeing of the people of the city, the government was granted the authority to enable the new zoning ordinances. The amalgamation of separation principles of Howard's Garden City model with the modernist's rationalist hierarchical model was adopted. This was a pivotal point in urban design history. It marked yet another change in the procedures used by urban professionals, a move away from urban 'plans' towards Euclidian zoning as a determinant of urban and suburban growth, shifting the emphasis away from plans, designs and urban form, to zoning, law, and land-use (Neuman 1998).

The term 'Euclidian Zoning', does not come directly from the Greek mathematician Euclid, it actually comes from the legal case of Village of Euclid v. Ambler Realty Co. (U.S. Supreme Court 1926) where the business Realty Co. who owned land in the town of Euclid Ohio in the United States, challenged the town planning zones which were in the process of being implemented, which sought to prohibit industrial uses on their site. The argument put forward by Ambler Realty Co's lawyers was that the zoning was 'unconstitutional', was dismissed in the supreme court with the verdict that the zoning was not an unreasonable extension of the village's police power, the 'power to regulate for the advancement of a community's health, morals, safety, or general welfare' (Burdette, 2004). This judgment immediately altered the position of the urban designer forever to one who would need to deal with the legalities of urbanism.

The zoning procedure, originally conceived to fulfil the urban desire for better living conditions, would have unforeseen effects on cities by encouraged urban sprawl and an innate fear of density.

God-given right to drive and park for free with 'ample parking day or night'...

One of the consequences of Euclidian zoning is that it seeks to create low-density communities and utilises large roadway networks and parking requirements to accomplish this. The zoning of the post–World War II era encouraged isolated 'pods' of single-land-use growth resulting in car-dependent urban environments that discouraged compact, mixed-use, energy-efficient development (Peirce 2006).

American critic of both zoning and urban sprawl, James Howard Kunstler suggest that 'sprawl involves a strict separation of human activities, mandatory driving, and huge supplies of free parking' (Kunstler, 1998). Kunstler speaks with disdain about Wall-Marts, and Victor Gruen conceived mega-shopping-malls that are scattered across the American landscape. Victor Gruen, a refugee from Austria, did not like the unsocial suburban lifestyle of 1950s America and wanted to design a community building type that was reminiscent of the arcades and plazas of Europe. He came up with the now universal model of the shopping mall, which was then surrounded by a vast sea of car parking. The result was probably not what he had in mind.

The phenomenon of urban sprawl is worldwide with the amount of area per capita consumed by spreading cities through Europe more than doubling during the last 50 years (Batty et al. 2003). The most notable examples of sprawl are, however, in the US and Australia. The Euclidian zoning response to community concerns for separation of land uses for health reasons, mixed with the new need to house returning soldiers and their families' 'baby boom', combining with access to inexpensive cars and cheap fuel, clever marketing of the detached dwelling 'American / Australian dream' and Federal road based infrastructure investments led to the wide adoption of 'urban sprawl'. Zoning and sprawl would become the centre of architectural and urban design debate for the next 65 years with predominantly a denial response of inaction continuing to this day.

> *Many of today's zoning and land-use regulations, building codes, and rules were written in response to public health and safety issues of a century ago, from tenement buildings without running water to slaughterhouses invading residential neighbourhoods. Today we're stuck with sterile zoning and restrictions on building materials and methods alarmingly out of sync with present-day needs (Peirce, 2006).*

To give a sense of the extent of denial inaction, we will discuss an example from Australia in the 1940s. During the last year of WWII in Melbourne, Barnett, Burt and Heath (1944) illustrated concerns for projected population growth and urban sprawl with the mapping of urban growth [Figure 18]. 'The increasing outward, uneven spread of the metropolis of Melbourne is a typical early sign of the overgrown, strangulated city so characteristic of old-world towns'. The authors then go on to advocate a city model of green wedges and a surrounding green belt. 'We must provide an agricultural belt, five miles wide to encircle the inner perimeter being approximately ten miles from the city's centre... Now is the time to do this... What a Godsend it would be to the future citizens of Melbourne'. They go on to talk about the cost of servicing the (then) outer suburbs, 'served by roads, and light and water and sewage at tremendous capital cost... The stupidity of it all! The inefficiency of it all! The ugliness of it all!' (Barnett et al., 1944).

The green wedge systems radiating from the centre mainly along existing waterways and creeks would terminate at the agricultural belt. Melbournians would be 'never more than 10 minutes' walk from a park, never more than 10 miles from the country' [Figure 19]. This vision for Melbourne was never to be fulfilled, though there are some remnants of the green wedges (those not filled by freeway now).

The questioning of sprawl as an appropriate mode of growth in Australia continued through the 1940s into the 50s and 60s by Melbourne architect and critic Robin Boyd with the scathing attack mainly on urban composition and aesthetics of suburbia, the pastiche of scattered tastelessness in the *Australian Ugliness* (Boyd, 1968), though this had little effect on the lateral spread of the city. The denial response continued.

Social segregation – denying the loss of diversity

Another symptom of loss that is being responded to with denial is the growing concern that different forms of urbanism can adversely impact on social equity (Dodson, Sipe, & Evans, 2008; R. Ewing, Hamidi, Grace, & Wei, 2016). Sprawling cities have ongoing problems with a lack of housing diversity. As Michael Batty and his colleagues at The Bartlett at University College London note, sprawl tends to segregate residential development according to income, which tends to exacerbate social and ethnic divisions. Hierarchical street layouts of cul-de-sacs and busy major roads also trap those who are very young and very old as they are unable to live effectively in such areas. The Euclidian zoning and sprawl

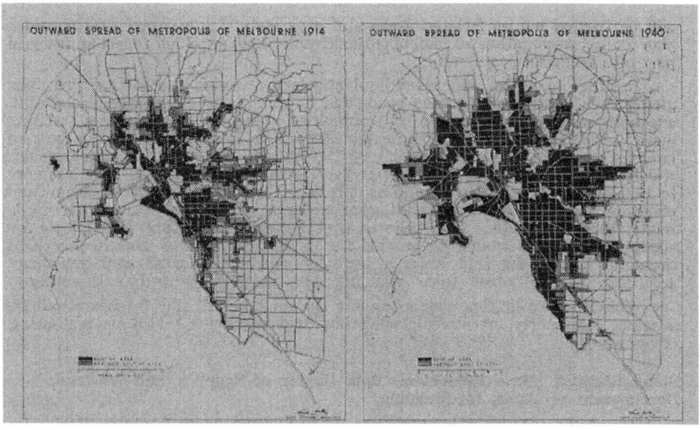

Figure 18: Outward spread of metropolis of Melbourne, source: We Must Go On - A Study Of Planned Reconstruction & Housing, (Barnett et al., 1944).

separate the poor from jobs, with minority groups at a significant disadvantage, in the US, particularly African Americans. Sprawl creates a concentration of the 'non-white' (Batty et al., 2003).

The long commute – denying the loss of time

The loss of time of populations due to long commutes in transit by car is another symptom that is also being responded to with denial. Since the end of WWII, Australian and US cities have given preference to funding road building over-investing in public transport. Road-biased funding, along with the lateral expansion of cities, has encouraged the increase of distances between homes, workplaces, schools and parks.

A study of comparative transport speeds in Canberra, Australia, by mathematician and environmental scientist Professor Paul Tranter centred upon 'effective speeds'¶¶ to compare different car models against public transport and cycling, found that cycling and public transport were by far faster than most medium-sized cars and considerably faster than the 4x4 (SUV) style 'land cruiser' when the time devoted to earning money needed to keep cars run-

---

¶¶ *Effective speed can be calculated using the formula: 'Speed = distance divided by time', where distance = the total kilometres travelled, and time is the total time devoted to the mode of transport (including the time spent at work to earn the money to pay all the costs created by the particular mode of transport).*

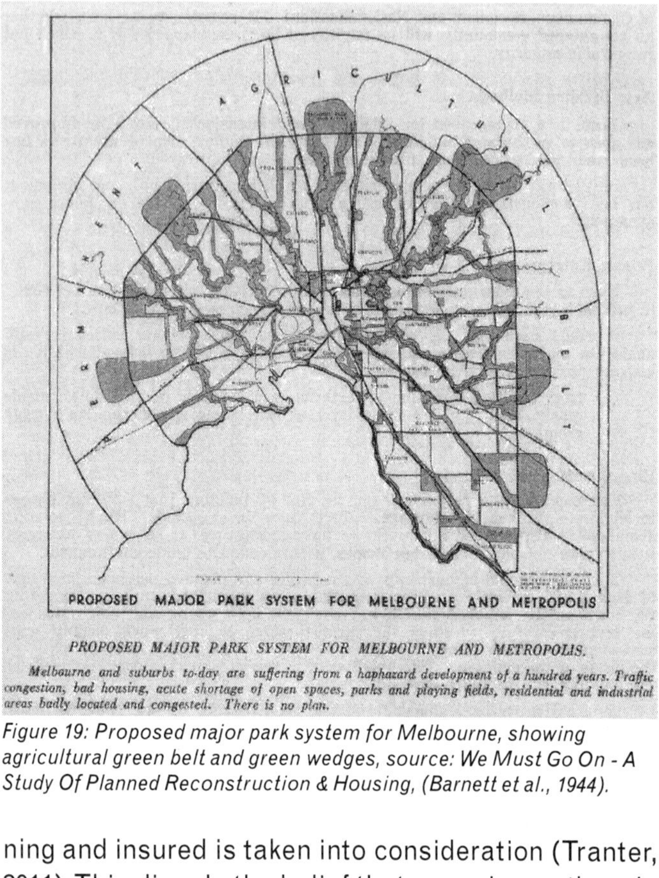

Figure 19: Proposed major park system for Melbourne, showing agricultural green belt and green wedges, source: We Must Go On - A Study Of Planned Reconstruction & Housing, (Barnett et al., 1944).

ning and insured is taken into consideration (Tranter, 2011). This dispels the belief that cars give us the advantage of high speed. The perceived freedom that a car brings is also brought under scrutiny as car drivers are 'entirely dependent on costly infrastructure, goods and services provided by a multitude of others'. Similarly, in the sprawling city of Los Angeles, the average motorist is delayed by between 74 and 93 hours each year in rush-hour traffic (Gorzelany, 2019; Schrank & Lomax, 2003). Eight out of ten Australians travel to and from work in their car, with an average commuting time per day of around one hour while about one in eight spends 90 minutes or more in their cars (S. Berry, 2016; ABS, 1996). Traffic congestion in Australian cities is estimated to cost over $16bn (AUD) through lost productivity (Shilton, 2016).

When a nation starts to lose the equivalent to a full working day each week sitting in their cars, it would appear that we have a pretty big problem. Unfortunately, the most common response to this problem, whilst in the stage of denial, is to build more freeway infrastructure. This response in itself is another denial of the 'induced demand' principle, which has been observed by transport researchers as early as the 1960s. In American economist Anthony Downs' publication, 'Law of Peak Hour Traffic Congestion', he concludes that 'on urban commuter expressways, peak-hour traffic congestion rises to meet maximum capacity' (Downs, 1962; Litman, 2019; Schneider, 2018). By considering commuter decision-making and its underlying set of assumptions, we can understand why building more freeways, does not result in reduced traffic congestion. To it put a different way, when you have dug yourself into a hole, the best response is to first recognise you are in a hole, secondly don't keep trying to convince yourself you are not in a hole, and thirdly, stop digging.

Obesity epidemic – denying the loss of health

Another symptom of loss that is being responded to with denial in contemporary society is the link between urban form and obesity. 'There is growing evidence not merely of correlation, but causation between sprawl, a lack of physical activity and major health problems such as obesity, diabetes and depression' (Kuiper 2006). Over 50% of short trips under 1km in Australian suburbs are by car (Charting Transport, 2014), and unsurprisingly, obesity rates in Australia are alarmingly high. Australia is fast closing the gap with the US for being the 'fattest nation in the world' (Lundy 2003) with physical inactivity estimated to cost the Nation's health budget several billion dollars annually (Shilton, 2016; Tolley, 2011).

These health concerns have encouraged a new kind of urban health research into the relationship between urban form, density, street layout, land-use, and obesity. Proving that denser cities with mixed uses within walking distance encourages walking, and therefore encourages better health, requires numerous large-scaled studies. One such study conducted in the US concluded that areas with more highly accessible gridded street networks that are more densely populated have higher health ratings than low density sprawled suburbs (Kelly-Schwartz, Stockard, Doyle, & Schlossberg, 2004). Another US study titled 'Obesity Relationships with Community Design, Physical Activity, and Time Spent in Cars' concluded:

> *Land-use mix had the strongest association with obesity [...]. Each additional hour spent in a car per day was associated with a 6% increase in the likelihood of obesity. Conversely, each additional kilometre walked per day was associated with a 4.8% reduction in the likelihood of obesity. [...] Strategies to increase land-use mix and distance walked while reducing time in a car can be effective as health interventions (Frank, Andresen, & Schmid, 2004).*

Similar conclusions have been made from other large-scale studies, even after controlling for observed confounding influences. Urban compactness measures are negatively related to BMI, obesity, heart disease, high blood pressure, and diabetes. People living in less sprawling places are likely to walk more, weigh less, and have a lower prevalence of hypertension than people living in cities with less compact development patterns. (R. Ewing, Meakins, Hamidi, & Nelson, 2014; McCann & Ewing, 2003).

Sprawl is perhaps the major problem facing urban planning at the beginning of the 21st century. It encapsulates the key problem of urban transportation which revolves around the emphasis on the car as the dominant means of movement (Batty et al., 2003).

As discussed in the previous chapter, urban desires for healthy cities continue, but today these health concerns are less about cholera, diarrhea, typhoid and the plague, contemporary concerns centre upon the obesity epidemic, along with related health problems such as diabetes and heart disease. This indicates that improving the fitness of the population is now a critical contemporary social aim and though nobody believes that these problems can be eradicated solely by urban design, the research suggests that it can have an impact. Greater population density and better urban connectivity should be high on the list of urban desires, but this will require populations and decision-makers to move past the stage of denial.

Second stage: Anger

‘it’s not fair... why me?’

Placing the blame (SOS, NIMBY & BANANA)

The second stage of dealing with loss is 'anger'. Here the patient moves on from not believing the diagnosis, to being angry that misfortune has been beset on them and not someone else and looks to place blame on others for the situation.

> *When the first stage of denial cannot be maintained any longer, it is replaced by feelings of anger, rage, envy, and resentment. The logical next question becomes: "Why me?" [...] why couldn't it have been him?' An old man whom I have known ever since I was a little kid came down the street. He was eighty-two years old [...] He's rheumatic, he's a cripple, he's dirty, just not the type of a person you would like to be. And the thought hit me strongly, now why couldn't it have been old George instead of me?" [...]. In contrast to the stage of denial, this stage of anger is very difficult to cope with from the point of view of family and staff. The reason for this is the fact that this anger is displaced in all directions and projected onto the environment at times almost at random (Kübler-Ross, 1973).*

Throughout the world, there are groups of residents

who are angry about any form of change within their immediate surrounding areas. Advocates of urban consolidation sometimes refer to these groups as NIMBY, which stands for Not in My Back Yard, or BANANA – Build Absolutely Nothing Anywhere Near Anything. NIMBYism is a term that became common during the 1980s to describe the opposition of community groups against change in their neighbourhood that might have even the remotest possibility of diminishing their home prices.

Many cities around the world have their own organised NIMBY densification resistance groups. As we are most familiar with the Australian context, in this section of the book, we will primarily explore Australian examples such as our local Save Our Suburbs (SOS) group, but we believe the examples will resonate with those from many other countries. We will also touch on some examples form the US and Europe.

The SOS group came to prominence in the mid-1990s. In 1993 the Victorian State Government introduced the *VicCode 2* regulations for medium density housing. These regulations were designed to increase urban consolidation and to reduce urban sprawl. It was met with angry resistance in politically sensitive streets of the conservative voting heartlands (Lewis, 1999). The recommendations for urban consolidation and increased population density for the greater good were met with fear and anger by existing residents, who believed that having to share their suburb and existing services with newcomers to the area would result in a loss of their amenity as existing property owners. Newcomers to existing inner suburbs in Melbourne are seen by some as 'parasitic' (Lewis, 1999), leeching the existing amenity of those who got there before them. 'The protection of amenity has been whittled away. In general quality and amenity controls [...] are set far too low to meet community expectations' (Lewis, 1999).

Though we think the labelling incoming community members as 'parasites' comes off a little strong, regarding the quality of development and amenity preservation, these fears may not be entirely without basis and are worthy of consideration. It is not unreasonable for the urban desires from post-industrial cities that we discussed in the first chapter for daylight and air movement to persist. Although the spread of typhoid and the plague are no longer the prime concern, the preservation of amenity is still an essential aspect of good urbanism.

Consolidation... the cause of housing affordability problems?

There exists a widely held belief that policies designed to contain urban growth by limiting the release of land for new development and encouraging urban consolidation, are what has been pushing housing prices up, causing the housing affordability crisis in most Australian cities.

Alan Moran, the former head of deregulation in the Institute of Public Affairs, a right-wing think tank with strong (angry) views against renewable energy suggests that 'the stellar rise in house prices across Australia was due to land prices and that 'those costs were shown to be derived from state governments and local authorities acting to restrict the availability of land for housing' (Moran, 2008; Costello & Rowley, 2010). By releasing more land' supply increases and thereby automatically leads to more affordable new land and housing. This sounds great. Just turn farmland into housing subdivisions on the outer edges of cities and the affordable housing problems are solved. Unfortunately, detailed studies documenting the impact of property prices where this approach has been implemented suggest that there is a *weak* relationship between house price growth and land supply (Costello & Rowley, 2010). As it turns out, it is a complete furphy that a lack of land release is the leading cause of increasing house prices. The prices are driven up by the relatively wealthy middle class with numerous properties, encouraged by overly generous tax incentives such as 'negative gearing' and reduced capital gains tax, that favour existing homeowners and investors in the marketplace.

Land releases have very little impact on affordability, particularly where housing locations are desirable in established and well-serviced suburbs. The argument of affordability also becomes extremely problematic when consideration for the commute time, cost of transport and the vulnerability of fuel costs are taken into account (Li, Dodson, & Sipe, 2018; Li, Sipe, & Dodson, 2016).

In a large-scale study by the Australian think tank, the Grattan Institute, of a wide range of policies aimed at *actually* improving housing affordability, it is suggested that boosting density in middle suburbs, though it is politically difficult (i.e. it is met with angry resistance), would have the highest impact on housing affordability in Australian cities (Daley, Coates, Wiltshire, & Grattan Institute, 2018).

It has also been suggested that the other pressure on housing prices actually comes from the NIMBY groups themselves due to their impact on local governments and their influence on housing policies. In the U.S., former Senator Mel Martinez (U.S. Secretary of Housing and Urban Development) stated, 'whether by intent—through the so-called NIMBY syndrome of exclusionary zoning, expensive building fees, and burdensome regulatory barriers—or unintentionally, local governments are driving up housing costs and driving out affordable housing'. Vital workers in our communities are being pushed farther and farther from the cities where they work by NIMBY opposition, resulting in greater sprawl, worse traffic congestion, and horrendous commutes in cities across the country (Duty & Tucker, 2006).

A common argument put forward by NIMBY and BANANA groups in opposition to densification is that 'people prefer not to live densely'. In North America, 'Fannie Mae'*** (Federal National Mortgage Association (FNMA) has been conducting surveys about housing preferences for decades. The findings have changed little over this time. Regardless of income, race or current tenure status, most citizens would prefer to live in a single-family home with a private yard. Of course, these results could be somewhat misleading as when asked 'would you prefer a house to flat' it assumes all else is equal. It is a bit like asking someone if they prefer really, really nice things or merely nice things. When citizens are pressed with more detailed questions they found the majority of people find many aspects of city life, such as the convenience of having shopping, schools, and public transportation within five to ten minutes of home 'very' or 'extremely appealing' and that, after making trade-offs between size and type of housing, and its location, people would prefer more compact housing in well serviced, denser neighbourhoods (FNMA, 1997; Kelly, Weidmann, & Walsh, 2011). Daley and Kelly found that when location and convenience trade-offs were considered by citizens, townhouses, semi-detached dwellings and apartments were con-

---

**** Fannie Mae is the colloquial name given to the Federal National Mortgage Association (FNMA) a government sponsored enterprise of the United States government used by researchers and professionals.*

sidered more desirable (Daley, Coates, & Wiltshire, 2017; Kelly et al., 2011). However, *The Housing We'd Choose* study conducted by the Grattan Institute revealed significant shortfalls in supply of these higher density housing types in well-serviced areas (2011).

Homeless advocate and director of San Francisco's Tenderloin Housing Clinic, Randy Shaw, has recently written the book, *Generation Priced Out: Who Gets to Live in the New Urban America* (2018), that examines how urban 'Boomer' homeowners, in their quest to fend off 'density' (and apartment renters) in their neighbourhoods, have consistently, and incredibly successfully, blocked the construction of affordable housing. Such NIMBYism has hindered the building of more housing in areas desirable to millennials, keeping stock low, prices high, and kept younger, less-affluent residents, as well as the working and middle classes more broadly, out of neighbourhoods. This is in stark contrast to the hypothesis of Jane Jacobs, who believed that preserving old buildings and stopping high density tower development would maintain population diversity and neighbourhood affordability. As Economics Professor at Harvard University, Edward Glaeser points out in his book *Triumph of the City* (2011). 'That is not how supply and demand work'. He goes on to advocate for high-rise housing renewal in existing urban areas, and provides historical evidence of New York City's subsequent price increases and impact overly pow-

Figure 20: 'Australia Full' bumper sticker on the back of a Holden Commodore car showing the attitude of fear and anger towards immigration and consolidation. Photograph: White, M.

erful historic-preservation groups had had on the city, including Jacobs' beloved West Village, which was a working-class neighbourhood when she lived there but has long since been transformed to be an exclusive gentrified part of the city.

Loss of space – 'Fuck off we're full'

Another expression of anger occurs when attempts to maintain business-as-usual denial are unsuccessful, and change begins to actually happen, that conflicts with people's ideas of what their future would be.

> *In middle and inner areas, unit developments are parasitic upon existing properties because their amenity is being destroyed, while units gain amenity at their expense... [units] strip part of the value from adjoining property... [including stealing] services and roads (Lewis 1999).*

Lewis' attitude towards sharing existing space and services is pervasive. The 'I got here first,' philosophy is in keeping with Australia's dubious past intolerance of perceived infringements on their Australian way of life[†††] [Figure 20].

Inner suburban areas of Greater Melbourne such as Hawthorn and Camberwell owned by predominantly middle upper-class whites have been ferociously protected from 'inappropriate development' by resident groups[‡‡‡] [Figure 21].

---

††† *White Australia policy restricted non-white immigration to Australia from 1901 to 1973. For further information on this, see James Jupp's From White Australia to Woomera: The Story of Australian Immigration (2002).*

‡‡‡ *By resident groups such as SOS and BRAG (Boroondara Resident's Action Group) https://www.facebook.com/Boroondara-Residents-Action-Group-1592337260978604/*

Figure 21: 'Boroondara-Full' digital artwork by Nulla Weinberg (2005). Satirical anti-immigration, anti-refugee, fear of Mexicans/Asians/ African Gangs art showing the attitude of fear and anger towards immigration and densification.

The Boroondara Council has the highest percentages of members of SOS (Lewis 1999), and also one of the highest rates of English speaking, Australian born residents (ABS 2006a). Higher density in the form of medium-density flats brings more migrants to communities, as occupants of medium density housing are predominantly not of Australian descent (ABS 1998).

At the risk of treading into Godwin's law territory[§§§], in an article '*How to Live With the NIMBY Syndrome*', writer for the *Ethical Spectacle*, Sy Schechtman, describes the ancient custom of

---

§§§ *Godwin's law, promulgated by the American attorney and author Mike Godwin, suggest that if a discussion (online) continues long enough, at some stage someone will compare someone or something to Adolf Hitler or the Nazis (Godwin, 1995). Generally, at this point the discussion ends.*

'nimbyism', and how the bible repeatedly advises the Jews to treat the stranger well, 'Remember, you were strangers in the land of Egypt.' (2003). He goes on to describe how nimbyism determined the fate of many Jews through the Second World War, describing the ship St. Louis, carrying around 1,000 Jewish refugees from Nazi Germany as the 'Ship of Fools'. Despite knowledge of their persecution, they were refused entry into Cuba, the United States, and other countries (Schechtman, 2003).

Recsei suggests capping populations and forming Ebenezer Howard-esque satellite new towns built adjacent to existing cities, developed to cater for a portion of the additional population that 'we have decided we need' that is of optimal size, with about 200,000 residents each (Recsei, 2004). Coincidently (?) there are examples of very similar approaches to dealing with population control and satellite growth can be found in Europe in the 1930s [Figure 22].

Though it is not explicitly discussed by SOS, there is a strong undercurrent of anti-immigration within their rhetoric. The President of SOS, when criticising urban consolidation, states:

> *The trouble is, Smart Growth is still growth. As more and more people come to live in that restricted area, up goes the population density... The Commonwealth government must take some responsibility. It cannot*

just assume, as it does now, that the States can forever shoehorn all new arrivals into existing communities... If we decide that our population has to increase [at all] (Recsei, 2004).

SOS advocates capping population growth, 'set a targeted limit to Sydney's population,' (Recsei 2004). This position of restricting growth is similar to other angry community members, represented by the member for Oxley in 1996, Pauline Hanson. In her maiden speech in parliament she recommended limiting immigration:

I believe we are in danger of being swamped by Asians. Between 1984 and 1995, 40% of all migrants coming into this country were of Asian origin. They have their own culture and religion, form ghettos and do not assimilate (Hanson 1996).

More recently, Hanson has shifted her position. No. Not to a more acceptance like support for a tolerant and inclusive multicultural society. She has just shifted the direction of her anger towards Muslims by now suggesting Australia is at risk of being 'swamped by Muslims' and telling those who are unwilling to adapt to the Australian way of life to 'go back to where you came from' (Norman, 2016).

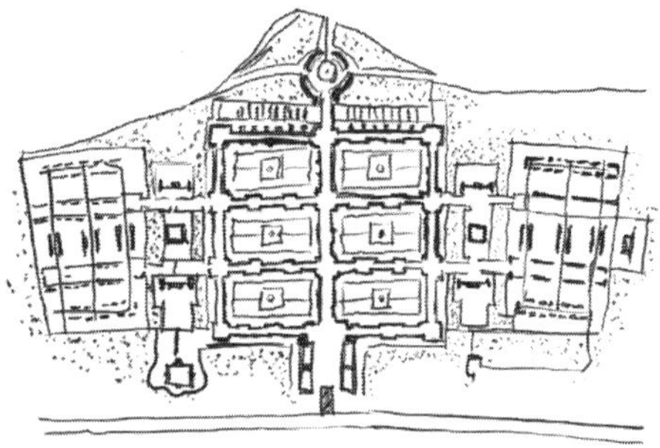

Figure 22: Lebensraum sketch by White, M. showing conceptualisation of a model National Socialist City satellite with a population of 200,000 people based on illustration in Architektur im Dritten Reich 1933-1945, (Teut, 1967).

Anger over energy costs - loss of global stability and reliance on foreign oil

In 1956 M. King Hubbert predicted that US oil production would peak around 1970, which turned out to be reasonably accurate (Witze, 2007). Further predictions using the same *Hubbert peak theory* have also been made globally, which suggest that world oil production will peak in the next few years. The geologist who worked with Hubbert, Kenneth S. Deffeyes argued that by as early as 2005, this peak may have already occurred (2006).

Over the last thirty years, numerous warnings about energy shortages and potential catastrophic impacts on cities have come from urban researchers. Predictions about the effects on cities that may be felt due to peak oil are likely to be exacerbated by increased demand for oil in China, the Middle East, and India, and may result in world turmoil, angry social upheaval, more wars for oil, and a radical re-thinking of what it will be like to live in the suburbs in the future.

At and IFHP conference in Copenhagen (2007), Professor Peter Newman, a leading researcher in environmental science and sustainability from Australia, presented an image from George Miller's 1981 classic *Mad Max 2* as an example of what post-peak oil outer suburbs may be like if immediate changes to the way people live are not made. In the film Max, played by Mel Gibson, travels around the Wasteland along with other scavengers in search of fuel, killing those with stockpiles. Newman comes to a similar conclusion about the consequences of oil dependence to that of North American author and social critic James Howard Kunstler:

> *We are not going to run Walmart, Walt Disney World, and the interstate highway system on hydrogen, coal synfuels, tar sand or oil shale distillates, biodiesel, ethanol, recycled french-fry oil, solar electricity, wind power, or nuclear fission. The stark truth of the situation is that we are simply going to have to make other arrangements – Suburbia will be coming off the menu (Kunstler 2005).*

The cities that will be hardest hit by peak oil will be those currently with the highest use and those with limited transportation options – the 'car-dependent' (Newman & Kenworthy 1989). U.S. cities are using four to six times the transport energy consumption of that used by western European cities and wealthy Asian cities. Even in cities in the Middle East, where much of the oil is produced, oil use is around a sixth of that of U.S. citizens (Kenworthy 2003). The cities with comprehensive public transport systems will be better prepared for peak oil as public transport 'only represents a fraction of total transport energy use, never exceeding 23% in any region regardless of the extent of service and usage' (Kenworthy 2003).

Of course, these warnings have predominantly gone unheeded with responses largely falling into the first stage denial category. There was, however, a glimpse into the possible *angry* future that can be triggered by energy shortages. On the 17th of October in 1973 the first 'oil crisis' began, when the members of OAPEC (Organization of Arab Petroleum Exporting Countries) decided that they would not export to nations that had supported Israel in the *Yom Kippur War* which included the United States and allies. By 1974, the price of oil quadrupled to nearly $12 (USD) per barrel. There were multiple reactions to this global energy crisis. We will return to some of the more positive responses of Scandinavia later in the book, but here we will stick with the more common one, which was extreme *anger*.

In the U.S., the oil shocks led to long lines at petrol pumps and absolutely irate motorists. It led to protests that continued into 1974, with truck drivers coordinating major strikes, garaging their rigs and blockading roads, with the result that commerce grinded to a halt. Angry protesters began to grow violent, with reported incidences of them dropping bricks off overpasses onto moving rigs (Williams, 2019). This was over forty years ago. Such anger wouldn't happen now though would it? Well, it doesn't take much to find recent examples of extreme anger over high fuel costs.

Last year in Paris, 3,000 French security forces and police were deployed, firing tear gas and spraying water cannons to disperse 280,000 people including violent demonstrators as they marched on the presidential Elysees Palace, staging road blockades to vent their anger against rising fuel taxes. They waved French flags as they set fire to burning barricades on the Champs-Elysees Avenue. 19 people, including four police officers, were injured, and over 100 arrests, were made (NBC, 2018).

Similar violent protests have also recently occurred in Mexico. Angry protesters blockaded highways, looted shops and forced service stations across Mexico to close after a 20% price increase on gasoline occurred (Agren, 2017). And this year, we have seen an even more extreme taste of the kind of angry response that may become more common with the protests that turned into deadly riots in Zimbabwe after petrol prices skyrocketed. In a bid to ease fuel shortages, the Government increased the cost of petrol by 150 per cent, resulting in strikes and protests that quickly escalated into riots with security forces firing tear gas into crowds and making 200 arrests. Several people were killed (Heanue, 2019).

Lucky we are moving to electric cars, so this won't be an issue in the future right? Well maybe. Assuming we can source enough cobalt for the lithium-ion battery electrodes which comes primarily from the Democratic Republic of the Congo (which hasn't exactly been the most stable place in the world), the car batteries will need to be charged somehow. It will require cities to maintain, or in most cases, upgrade struggling power grid infrastructure to meet increased charging load demands. There will be other challenges to do with power generation, given much of grid power comes from dirty sources like burning coal, oil, and gas. So, unless you are in Norway where almost all electricity is generated from renewable resources, electric cars will be powered primarily by a mix of coal and oil. No worries, there is plenty of coal to keep digging up in countries like Australia and the US, and their political leaders are very keen to keep building new mines so they can export the stuff, right? Again, yes... that is currently the case, but those who saw Greta Thunberg's speech at the United Nations Climate Summit at the UN Headquarters in New York, that may no longer be the case pretty soon. It was pretty clear that Thunberg was not in the denial stage and was very much in the anger stage when she said 'We will never forgive you. We will not let you get away with this'. If Thunberg is the spokesperson for this younger generation around the world, (she is, at least according to these author's own children), then in a few years from now not only will the coal be staying in the ground, but trials for environmental crimes against humanity will be being held.

Hopefully, all these issues about electric energy generation and storage can be worked out soon, as, like the petroleum riots we mentioned were occurring recently, we have also begun to see angry and violent clashes in the Armenian capital against rising electricity prices (Luhn, 2015) and energy price protests happening in France (Gordon, 2019).

Procedures of media saturation and viral marketing

Before we move on from anger to the next stage of grief, let us return to the anti-consolidation NIMBY and BANANA groups and touch on some of their methods. The procedures used by these groups of the 'anger paradigm' are of interest in that they tapped into what we now call social media very early on. NIMBY and BANANA groups have been very effective at lobbying governments through the use of mass media, webpages, email and now social media platforms such as Facebook.

The Australian example of SOS makes use of the internet with websites such as www.sos.org.au, which share information such as different state organisations; information about recent planning policy changes; links to SOS propaganda videos on YouTube (such as www.youtube.com/user/Wildhiland), as well as pro-sprawl websites such as www.demographia.comThere are also instructions on the website advising residents on how to restrict urban consolidation in their areas by objecting to projects in planning. A recent example is the *Residents Guide to Objecting* (Davenport, 2016), which sets out arguments for objecting to any kind of development that 'experience has shown' to be effective. The document has a section called 'Maximise your objection with Council' and lists effective arguments for objecting to most proposals such as to argue that the 'height and mass/bulk are visually unacceptable'; 'the proposed development does not integrate with the neighbourhood character. Important characteristics include roof form, building height, building materials, landscape and fencing'; or that 'the density of the development is excessive.'

Third stage: Bargaining

‘a vain hope that the bad news is reversible’

New New Urbanism Final Final 2

The next stage of dealing with grief is 'bargaining'. The bargaining stage is where one holds onto a vain hope that the bad news is reversible and that by making promises of good behaviour, one can go back to how things were before the bad news. Just like the child whose parents deny their request to see the Logan X-Men (R-rated) movie, starts to brush their teeth and promises to keep their room from getting *'messy'* without being asked, hoping to change the outcome of the decision, terminal patients in the bargaining stage might promise to God that they will 'never smoke again', 'go to church every Sunday from now on', 'walk to work instead of driving', 'trade booze and drugs for a clean and wholesome, traditional lifestyle' or even 'be polite to their mother-in-law'.

> *If we have been unable to face the sad facts in the first period and have been angry at people and God in the second phase, maybe we can succeed in entering into some sort of an agreement which may postpone the inevitable happening: "If God has decided to take us from this earth and he did not respond to my angry pleas, he may be more favourable if I ask nicely" (Kübler-Ross, 1973).*

We suggest that the urban design movement, 'New Urbanism'¶¶¶ belongs to this stage. Formerly known as 'Traditional Neighbourhood Development,' or 'Neo-traditionalist', New Urbanism is an articulated resistance to messy uncontrolled urban sprawl and to modern city planning (Loomis 1999).

In this chapter, we will discuss how the movement mixes nostalgic yearning for the past with promises of good urban behaviour (for example, promising to keep their city from being messy) and explore New Urbanism 'bargaining town' examples in the U.S., the U.K., Australia and China.

New Urbanism grew predominantly in the United States in the 1980s out of a postmodern critique of modernist urbanism. The movement was built on observations by American writers such as Kevin Lynch, Colin Rowe, Jane Jacobs, Christopher Alexander and the work of European architects Leon and Rob Krier. In an attempt to reverse the loss of the old city, the non-referential buildings of the modernist movement that had been the target of much anger, and the undesirable effects of endless sprawling no-place,

---

¶¶¶ *The 'New Urbanism' names feels ironic, as the paradigm is focused on the past, but also problematic in terms of design nomenclature. As most computer-geek contemporary architects know, when naming anything, for example a CAD file, it is poor practice to use words like 'new' or 'latest' as part of the name (eg. New-plan.dwg), as files are inevitably updated or revised, leading to renaming the file 'new-new-plan.dwg', or 'new-new-plan-final.dwg.*

this urban design movement emphasises 'traditional' design elements. Drawing upon Kevin Lynch's *The Image of the City* (1960), in which he described the physical form of the traditional city as being made up of five elements: paths, edges, districts, nodes and landmarks. The movement emphasises public plazas, terminating vistas (like those we explored in the *Pretty City* discussion earlier), and historical housing styles. It aims to shift the emphasis of the street from the car to the pedestrian, by the de-emphasis of street hierarchy in favour of 'traditional' street layouts.

The first book in Duany Plater-Zyberk's (DPZ) list of 'Books Essential to the New Urbanism' is Christopher Alexander's, *A Pattern Language* (1977), *which is described* as the 'The design equivalent of the Bible'. The book illustrates around 250 unitary patterns from traditional architecture, and sets out rules for traditional design. Alexander calls each spatial region a 'centre', emphasising that it is not an isolated entity, but an embedded field within an infinitely larger system of fields with gradually diminishing contextual influences. One cannot look at a part of the whole without looking at its relation to the whole, and the complex influences of its location within the field (Mehaffy, 2004). In a similar vein, the group of New Urbanists called the Congress of New Urbanism (CNU), has set out the 'Charter for New Urbanism' with a total of 27 key principles or *prom-*

ises for urban design, under the fields, '*The block*: the street, and the building', '*The neighbourhood*: the district, and the corridor' and '*The region*: Metropolis, city, and town'. Like the dying patient bargaining with promises of good behaviour to try to reach an agreement with God in order to postpone the inevitable, the charter bargains with *principle/promises* of good-behaviour progressivism, with some quite regressive historicism heavily sprinkled with a nostalgic yearning for the good ol' days. Some of the fundamental principle/promises from the CNU Charter include: maintaining urban growth boundaries; encouraging brownfield infill development; maximising connectivity for transit, pedestrian, and bicycle systems to maximize access and mobility throughout the region while reducing dependence upon the automobile; compact mixed-use development; affordable housing with a broad range of housing types and price levels to attract people of diverse ages, races, and incomes; Transport Oriented Development (TOD); and distinctive form for Civic buildings (CNU, 2015). These principles, in principle, sound quite reasonable and very much appear consistent with the good behaviour promises of the Bargaining Stage. It is, however, in the implementation and slightly unhealthy desire for the good ol' days where the movement becomes somewhat problematic.

This movement was beginning at a time when, as the Professor of Sustainable Urbanism at the University of Westminster, Michael Neuman points out, lawyers and planners had replaced designers and engineers as the leading professionals shaping urban growth policy, reflecting a shift from designs to words (1998). In contrast, New Urbanists put forward comprehensive visions, clearly illustrated with plans and perspective views of expected architectural outcomes. However, their representation methods were deliberately archaic, using pencil and watercolours to give drawings a 'historical' or 'timeless' feel, whilst the looseness of the non-ruled linework also suggests a sort of freedom.

Make America Great Again with New Urbanism?

Eric Owen Moss of EOM architects in California talks about the input of New Urbanism in the Hurricane Katrina rebuilding with scepticism, suggesting it is 'right-wing developer-speak masquerading as populism [...]The ideological image-making that would appeal to a kind of anachronistic Mississippi that yearns for the good old days of the Old South as slow and balanced and pleasing and breezy, and each person knew his or her role' (Hales, 2005).

> *Do you remember when women weren't allowed to vote, and certain folk weren't allowed on golf courses? Petridge Farm remembers... [from Futurama] (Verrone, 1999).*

In North America, a well-known built example of New Urbanism is 'Seaside', Florida. Built on the coast of the Gulf of Mexico in 1982, DPZ designed the new town embracing historical styles of the American South, concepts of walkability and civic vistas. The project is noteworthy as one of 'reviving the plan' clearly articulating a comprehensive vision for the development (Neuman, 1998). The resulting development has a strange newly built ye-olde look with a folksy architectural style, and an eerie cleanness that makes it appear almost like a real town, but not quite – a kind of uncanny valley urban fabric [Figure 23].

This somewhat creepy built outcome of the 'Seaside' development was exploited in *The Truman Show* film, the 1998 fantasy comedy directed by Peter Weir, written by Andrew Niccol. In the film the central character, Truman Burbank, played by Jim Carrey, lives in a constructed reality for the entertainment of those outside in a fake town called *Seahaven*. Truman is surrounded by actors playing the roles of folksy idealised citizens, pretending to have friendly relationships with him whilst going about their fabricated business and occasional segues into product-placement beer commercials. The simulated friendly neighbourhood citizens mimic the simulated friendly wholesomeness of Seaside's idealised urban set-like historical mimicry architecture. There is an additional layer of strangeness to this storey.

Figure 23: Photogrammetry point-cloud aerial view of the new town of Seaside, Florida, by Andrés Duany & Elizabeth Plater-Zyberk (DPZ), 1982, map data: Google, Landsat/Copernicus.

While the town of Seaside appears to have been chosen sardonically as the set for *The Trueman Show* because of its strange inauthenticity or fakeness, in the twenty years since the movie's theatrical release, the Seaside township has embraced the film, proudly renaming 31 Natchez Street, the main protagonist's home in Seaside (Seahaven), *The Truman House*.

When we look at the actual (real) town, Seaside village appears walkable and compact, but in reality, it is also swamped with cars that make it a challenge to move around. The township is suffering from the effects of climate change. It is battered by hurricanes and has lost so much of the primary and tertiary dunes that houses closest to the ocean are in danger of being subsumed by erosion. Despite the intention for a mix of affordable housing types within walking distance to workplaces, the township has also 'failed miserably at maintaining affordable housing stock' and has 'no industry to speak of, except for tourism' (Bernstein, 2005).

Seaside has all the authenticity of South Park's social commentary on wholesome *hipster gentrification* explored by Trey Parker and Matt Stone's 19th season of South Park 2015[****]. In the words of the Whole Foods representative to Randy Marsh, the character who had been lobbying for the towns very own natural and organic supermarket, 'I've never seen a town put so much energy into displaying an exaggerated sense of social consciousness' (Jeffries, 2015).

The Princely pomp of Poundbury in the UK

In the late 1980s, the European architect Leon Krier was commissioned by the Prince of Wales to design the village of Poundbury, a new town in Dorset, UK. Prince Charles is well known for his anti-modern, anti-contemporary architecture stance and directed the town to be designed according to 'traditional' planning methods with Neo-Georgian and traditional Germanic architectural styles. Strict design controls were set up to ensure stylistic consistency during the construction, which began in 1993. This stylistic

**** *The entire 19th season of South Park is worth watching for anyone interested in urban renewal, the continuing impact of Jane Jacobs, and to see how the pitfalls of gentrification play out.*

control sterilises any contamination of contemporary aesthetics that may have crept in. The resulting new town is 'dressed up' in its *ye-olde* style but is glib and is even more eerie than the Seaside example, perhaps because of the UK weather (and not being next to a beach). It has a feel of the young Norman Bates wearing his mother's old-fashioned clothing on his way to visit the shower.

Though limited in the mix of land uses with predominantly residential properties, Poundbury appears successful in creating a cycle-friendly environment with a short ride to the nearby township of Dorchester, made more comfortable and cycle-friendly as the streets appear almost abandoned without much in the way of pedestrian or vehicular movement most of the time.

Town building is no Mickey-Mouse operation – 'Celebration'

An equally well-known New Urbanist development designed by Robert Stern for Disney™, in 1996 was called 'Celebration' at the edge of 'Walt Disney World' in California, designed in a similar vein to Poundbury and Seaside but with even stricter control over aesthetics. There is a limited palette of housing styles from which residents are allowed to choose, and on existing houses, permission is needed before any colour or plant is changed. With a population of 1500, intended to eventually reach 20,000, the development has been a financial success though unforeseen social problems have occurred. Four years after opening the school, Celebration schoolteachers, administrators, and executives of Disney's Celebration Company were plagued by turmoil. The Celebration kindergarten-through-12th grade approach and experimental teaching syllabus led to a situation where many families transferred their children to other schools and many packed up and left town (Frantz, 1999).

An analysis of the New Urbanist Disney town Celebration, by Michael Pollan's in the *New York Times* titled; 'Town Building is No Mickey-Mouse Operation,' (1997), suggested that Disney's expertise was in building theme parks for paying guests, not towns for 'chaotic', 'ever-changing' and 'inevitably political' real citizens, concluding that these three human traits pretty much sum up everything the culture of Disney cannot abide'.

Though there is support from both the political left and right, New Urbanism also receives criticism from both sides. Criticism from the right suggests that New Urbanism is too paternalistic, that the free market should decide the urban form, that it is anti-capitalist, therefore anti-democratic; and that it 'embraces pie-in-the-sky social engineering based on a false diagnosis of society's urban problems'. The left criticises the authoritarian nature of stylistic limitations and the built examples of New Urbanism's failure to address one of the charter's critical objectives for affordability. Instead of producing a broad range of housing types at different price levels bringing people of diverse ages, races, and incomes into daily interaction, the towns are turning out to be 'rather elitist settlements with average income levels much higher than in the surrounding areas' (Gordon & Richardson 1998).

As well as appealing to the political and social right, the imagery that the strict aesthetic controls produce in New Urbanist towns and architecture in the bargaining promise 'not to be messy', can, according to architect and theorist Peter Eisenman, lead to blandness and the 'kind of repression that exists in the notion of a classical architecture' (1989). This 'blandness' occurs despite New Urbanist's deliberate reaction *against* the rationalist aesthetics of the Modernists before them, who they criticise for their minimalist aesthetics and 'blandness'.

The Kensington Banks... Oh so SoDoSoPa

New Urbanism encourages increased density within walking distance of transit, promotes walkable streets with pedestrian safety at the forefront of design. An example of this New Urbanism implementation can be found in the Australian suburb of Kensington Banks in Melbourne's inner North-West. Constructed in the early 1990s, the housing development's planning makes a solid attempt at pedestrian prioritisation with a layout that features vehicular cul-de-sacs, permeability for pedestrians and cyclists. The street network focuses upon the central public open space surrounded by 'The Crescent' – which is literally a scaled-down version of the Royal Crescent in Bath but constructed from lightweight timber framing with 10-millimetre thick cement sheet and a rendered finish which started to crack at the sheet joints shortly after construction was complete.

The preference for 'brownfield' development over greenfield growth at the suburban fringe is commended by environmentalists due to its reclamation of disused sites within urban growth boundaries. The designers believed that the retention of elements of the existing urban fabric would provide a sense of history and authenticity to the site. Built on a former livestock saleyards, abattoir and army depot, elements of the old land uses have been retained in the Kensington Banks development. New Redgum sleeper fencing runs along the old bluestone stock route that was used to run cattle and sheep from the holding yard at Newell's Paddock to the East, past the Glue and By-products Pty Ltd factory up through the saleyards and abattoir, and the original saleyards administration office building was retained and converted into a community school [Figure 24].

To the cynical, this New Urbanism promise to be authentic through retention of the old, is just another marketing ploy aimed at unauthentic segmentation of buyers according to aesthetic tastes to sell more

Figure 24: Photogrammetry point-cloud aerial view of Kensington Banks map data: Google, Landsat/Copernicus.

houses (Ford 1999). Rather than authenticity this retention of the old urban grain becomes marketing exploitation, as poignantly explored in the 19th season of South Park (Parker, 2015). The third episode, 'The City Part of Town', explores the redevelopment of the area surrounding Kenny McCormick's run-down family home titled 'South of Downtown South Park' or *SoDoSoPa*. The episode includes advertisements for 'The Residences at the Lofts at SoDoSoPa' which feature live-action video footage collaged with South Park animated cartoons. The development is marketed as 'presenting the rustic charm of a mixed-income crowd' [cuts to the dirt-poor Kenny and his father who can't afford to buy the

$10 ice-creams] and 'featuring state of the art architectural finishes with views of the Historic Kenny's house'. The 'Residences at the Lofts' is strikingly similar to 'The Vue Apartments' at the North-East edge of Kensington Banks that overlook the 'rustic charm' of the stock route and the 'mixed urban grain' with distant social housing beyond the edge of the New Urban precinct [Figure 24].

Though the intentions of preserving elements of existing urban fabric are not necessarily bad – and retaining elements of the old buildings and infrastructure does indeed provide a mixed urban grain, the combination of actually old structures with the newly constructed ye-olde styled housing is problematic at Kensington Banks. The development echoes the monotony of its New Urban friends on the other side of the world. The fake ye-olde, millimetres thick nostalgic rendered façade treatments of the new buildings water down the impact of the truly old structures of the original stockyards built one hundred or so years ago, giving the appearance that *all* of the buildings, including those from the original stockyard, were built in the early 1990s.

New Urbanism and the 'New Right' aesthetics

According to Leon Krier, New Urbanist principles promise 'simplicity and practicality of moral precepts less prescriptive than they are permissive', avoiding the tyrannical sophistications of utopian reform (Salingaros 2001). This 'permissive yet prescriptive' model of urbanism enforces historical styles which, as we highlighted earlier, appeal greatly to the political and social right leading to some of the movement's biggest criticisms. In his book *Success in the Art of Prediction, Architecture 2000 and Beyond* (initially published in 1969), Charles Jencks predicted a right-wing neo-classical revival resembling what Philip Johnson described as a 'new craving for monumentality' under the Nazis, would occur in the United States 'around 1984' (Jencks, 2000).

According to assistant professor Michael Kaplan, from Indiana University, Andres Duany (DPZ) acknowledges:

> *German town planning during the Third Reich as one of his sources of inspiration. Seaside, with its authoritarian building code and derivative style is, in the end, a scheme for the affluent by an enterprising private developer, hardly a paradigm for socially responsive urban development (Kaplan, 1995).*

With the risk of again proving Godwin's law, the comparison between New Urbanism and the Third Reich's urban design is not unfounded. New towns of 'Herman Goering Werke' at Salzgitter founded in 1938 as Stadt des KdF-Wagens ('City of the KdF

Car' now Wolfsburg), like the New Urbanist designs, 'stressed neo-classical design patterns in the new community settlement and a need for unity through building (Einigung), romanticism, mediaeval settlement patterns' (Mullin, 1982). In the context of this discussion, it is fitting to detour again to mention a particularly interesting example in the spread of New Urbanism that goes as far as China. The Anting New Town is a German-ish emergence of New Urbanism within the 'One City, Nine Towns-Plan' Shanghai satellite city development. The proposal for the Nine Towns-Plan is conceptually very interesting, transplanting historic European city forms into the rapidly expanding Chinese urban landscape. Anting, a Frankfurt-based architectural and planning firm has designed a simulated traditional German-style township modelled after the city of Weimar, less than an hour from central Shanghai. The architects – Albert Speer & Partners (AS&P). You may be thinking – Albert Speer, wasn't he Hitler's architect and Minister of Armaments? 'The Partners' must be referring to Goebbels and Himmler? No. AS&P was founded by Albert Speer Jr, the son of the 'Devil's Architect'. Speer Jr., who preferred not to be compared to his father (but didn't change his name for some reason?), designed and implemented an organic medieval European town layout, with strict quality control over the construction of buildings within the city.

The resulting city delivers on its promises of

exceptionally high construction quality, high energy efficiency, waste minimisation and separation, a generous supply of public open spaces, permeable street layout with short distance walks to services and a stylistically pure and consistent 'clean' overall aesthetic. To be fair to Speer Jr., the building aesthetics depart somewhat from the traditional German styling and are generally closer to Gropius and the Bauhaus than the grotesque neo-classicism of Speer's father. There are some strange mistranslations of traditional Germanic cities in the urban morphology too. The road network, though maintaining reasonably small block sizes, is not exactly what you would call 'walk-friendly', with typical contemporary Chinese road-widths even into the centre of town. We suspect the development suffers from the Shanghai car-prioritisation planning codes here. The overly broad streets betray the new-ye-olde attempt at walkable medieval-city connectivity whilst exaggerating the sense of emptiness contributing to the 'ghost-town' feel. This emptiness is also due to the underoccupancy of so many of the dwellings. Anting is one of the many Chinese 'ghost-towns' resulting from rampant over-speculation. Like the surrounding developments in different European country styles, the development has found it challenging to attract the expected tenants and, other than tourists and occasional wedding couples posing for photographs, appears mostly unoccupied.

Nostalgia just ain't what it used to be...

The New Urbanism paradigm expresses a yearning for the past – before the bad news. There are bargaining promises of progressive urban thinking that are made, and to some extent, are fulfilled by many of the built New Urbanist examples. The projects are definitely more liveable than the business as usual sprawling denial, with higher densities, healthier active transport considerations with better pedestrian connectivity and mix of land-uses that are concentrated close to public transit nodes. But the aesthetic fixation upon nostalgic architectural styling of the prettier past is a tad cheesy, and is rarely done in a way that is convincing, even as a remake. The styles push the nostalgia buttons but are inferior copies that don't hold a candle to the originals. They feel like George Lucas' Star Wars Prequels which rely very heavily upon nostalgia to propel their thin, childish plots and cover for Hayden Christensen's dreadfully lifeless acting. Just like The Phantom Menace relies on familiarity with the appearance of C3PO and life partner R2D2, New Urban towns require gabled rooves and porticos to mask their equally lifeless and stylistically monotonous drudgery.

Interestingly, the New Urbanist towns like Anting flopped in China just like the Star Wars Prequels. We posit this is, at least in part, for the same reason.

The Prequels relied heavily upon fan's nostalgia for the original film from the 1970s, but this was prior to Deng Xiaoping announcing the 'open door policy', so the Chinese movie-going public was not exposed to the original Star Wars. They, therefore, did not have the strength of nostalgia required to grit their way through Christensen delivering his 'I don't like sand... it's coarse and rough and irritating, and it gets everywhere' line to get to the lightsabre battles featuring a spritely fan-favourite Yoda. They really didn't know Yoda and friends, and so the Prequels tanked at the Chinese box office. It would seem that Anting suffers a similar fate due to the transplanted nature of its nostalgia. The Chinese property buying public is not intimately familiar with traditional European cities and therefore does not have the same level of nostalgia that is felt by citizens in the UK, North America or Australia. The traditional European styles don't appease a benign yearning for a simpler time when children did not require 5 Volt power connections to be happy, nor the desires for the old times when labour was very, very cheap. In the longer term, with the rise of the middle class and ability to travel, more Chinese citizens may holiday to the original urban landscapes upon which these new towns are based, and they may experience the kind of nostalgia one gets thinking about holidays in faraway places and then these towns may eventually become a roaring success.

Fourth stage: Depression

'I'm so sad, why bother?'

The next stage of grief is 'depression'. One urban design position sometimes referred to as 'Post Urban', is that described by architect Rem Koolhaas of the Office of Metropolitan Architecture (OMA). When Koolhaas states that urbanism is dead and that the uncontrollable generic city has taken over (Koolhaas & Mau, 1995), he is suggesting that there is no longer hope in achieving urban coherence or unity in any way and that it is futile to try. American architect Mark Gilbert suggests that the Koolhaas rhetoric brings to mind Shakespeare's Mark Anthony: 'he is here to bury the city, not to praise it' (2003).

> *When the terminally ill patient can no longer deny his illness, when he is forced to undergo more surgery or hospitalization, when he begins to have more symptoms or becomes weaker and thinner, he cannot smile it off anymore. His numbness or stoicism, his anger and rage will soon be replaced with a sense of great loss. This loss may have many facets: a woman with breast cancer may react to the loss of her figure; a woman with a cancer of the uterus may feel that she is no longer a woman (Kübler-Ross, 1973).*

Koolhaas suggests that the ability of architects to

impact on the built environment and on people's lives is grossly overestimated and that much of the criticism of the Modernist architects is misplaced.

> *There is an unbelievable overestimation of the power of architecture in the terms of [the] good it can do, but even more in the terms of [the] bad it can do or can't do. Architects have been instrumental in this assessment through their accusation of modern architecture. In the various complaints and criticisms that they developed during the 60s and 70s, and in the howling wolves against the imagined misdeeds of modernism, I think architects in a very important way have weakened their own profession (Koolhaas & Mau, 1995).*

For the latter half of the 20th century, the impact of architects has been minimal on urbanism, no longer acting as urban surgeons making grand civic gestures or building large scale expressions of new experimental healthy urban typologies. The most dramatic effects on urban form have been driven by traffic management, statutory planners (those who set up the land use zones), and real-estate developers who use nostalgia as a marketing tool to enable the denial and bargaining discussed in the previous chapters.

[The generic city is a] displacement to the urban periphery, a territory that can no longer be called suburbia, distorted and stretched beyond precedent, big enough for all [...] (Koolhaas & Mau, 1995).

Koolhaas suggested that urban sprawl is un-tameable, urban designers should not even try, and should 'run with it and go along for the ride' (Mehaffy, 2004). This position of post-urban hopelessness concerning the urban realm and the retreat into creating 'more or less masterful buildings' is very much a symptom of depression. We posit this depression stage is the forerunner to the 'Starchitect' phenomena of the late 1990s onwards and is a manifestation of grief that is 'reactive depression' (Kübler-Ross, 1973) that relates to an individual's self-esteem.

Depressed starchitects

I'm so depressed I will just do pretty things/objects/blobjects/landscapes/parametric urbanism

'Starchitect' is a term given to architects who have risen to a semi-celebrity status and are known by the general public for iconic 'masterful buildings'. Among the well-known starchitects are Rem Koolhaas, Zaha Hadid, Daniel Libeskind, Greg Lynn and Norman Foster, with perhaps the best-known starchitect, the American, Frank O Gehry who has even appeared in the popular television series, *The Simpsons,* in the episode 'The Seven-Beer Snitch'. During this Simpsons episode, the fourteenth of season sixteen in 2005, Marge writes to Frank Gehry asking him to design a new cultural centre for Springfield. Totally disinterested in working on a building in a tiny, uncultured red-neck North American township, Gehry screws up the letter throwing it on the ground, then looks at the paper and decides to design the building using the screwed-up paper as the masterful building form. Of course, it turned out that upon completion of the dazzling masterpiece of architecture, Springfield was not really interested in high-cultural activities and the building fell into disrepair until it was repurposed as a privately-run prison. The episode played upon the many similar projects done by Gehry that came after his well-known project – the Guggenheim Museum in Bilbao, Spain.

The Guggenheim, completed in 1997, expresses the depressive abandonment of pushing boundaries of art exhibition, in contrast to Frank Lloyd Wright's Guggenheim in NYC where the art is displayed upon a downwardly spiralling helix on curved walls with a slight backwards lean to display the artwork as though it was 'still on the artist's easel'. In Bilbao, the art is presented in a fairly conventional, flexible gallery arrangement – not dissimilar to any generic art gallery built in recent decades. Gehry's energy was very much focused upon the formal expression and pushing the boundaries of parametric building information modelling and innovative construction procedures.

Despite the design seeming to abandon any perceivable response to the urban context, the building was like a piece of urban alchemy that dramatically contributed to recovery from Bilbao's late 20th Century industrial decline. It increased the level of tourism for the city significantly as the world's artists, architects, and wannabe architects flocked in their thousands to the city to see the dazzling, titanium-clad piece of gratuitous formal gymnastics. This urban alchemy became known as the 'Guggenheim effect' and has been sought to be replicated by cities the world over since with varying degrees of success, but never quite as triumphantly as the Bilbao example.

The building designs of starchitects such as Gehry and Koolhaas, have received considerable criticism as they tend to operate as 'lone geniuses' contributing a monologue - often an urbanistically selfish one, with buildings said to be stylistically sensational, merely attempting to shock or wow the onlooker, and not integrate into the broader urban context (Kelbaugh, 2000). The buildings do not attempt to blend with a historic local identity, urban theories based upon history, typology, contextualism, believing that identity conceived as this form of sharing the past is a losing proposition. Despite being criticised for ignoring and overpowering any local discourse, Gehry describes his exuberant insertions into the city as 'examples of open, democratic urbanism', that encapsulate a sense of freedom and architectural expression. This expressive freedom is contrasted with the experimental typologies, programmatic influence and formal control entrusted to the Modernist architects.

Another example of expressive starchitectural attraction success is the Vitra Campus in Weil am Rhein, Germany, close to Basel, Switzerland [Figure 25]. Here, a murder[††††] of depressed starchitects congregates for an architectural battle royal the likes of which have not seen since the Weißenhofsiedlung in Stuttgart in 1927. In recent decades the Swiss furniture manufacturer Vitra has developed a campus of heroic architectural works that draw design and architecture tourists from around the world. The campus pre-dates the Bilbao Guggenheim with early work by Nicolas Grimshaw in 1981, followed by work by many others including Tadao Ando and Zaha Hadid in 1993, Renzo Piano 2013 and Herzog and de Meuron in 2018. The Vitra Campus also includes a prelude to the Guggenheim with a foray into blobjects by Frank Gehry in 1989 with both the Vitra

†††† *We suggest a 'murder' is a better collective noun for a group of architects than 'argument of architects' given the thematic context of this book and their predilection for wearing black.*

Figure 25: Photogrammetry point-cloud aerial view of the Vitra Campus in Weil am Rhein, Germany, map data: Google, Landsat/Copernicus.

design Museum building which embraces expressive curves that would dominate his later work, and the more decorative façade elements of the Vitra Factory Building, a conventional rectangular, flat-roofed factory with 'bolt-on architectural' elements. These bolt-on elements are of a cosmetic surgical augmentation nature, and like other above examples, does not push boundaries with typological nor programmatic experimentation, choosing instead to apply a slight three-dimensional distortion or decoration of the familiar.

Pre-post-mortem cosmetology – skin jobs and green jobs

This leads us to pre post-mortem cosmetology – skin jobs. Kübler-Ross describes a patient with terminal cancer who had great faith in Christian Science and held onto this belief to the last day. Despite this persistent aspect of the denial stage, she had faced reality enough to be hospitalised and receive some real treatment.

> *As she grew weaker, her make-up became more grotesque. Originally rather discreetly applied red lipstick and rouge, the makeup became brighter and redder until she resembled a clown. Her clothing became equally brighter and more colorful as her end approached. During the last few days she avoided looking in a mirror, but continued to apply the masquerade in an attempt to cover up her increasing depression and her rapidly deteriorating looks (Kübler-Ross, 1973).*

This attempt to coverup the increasing depression and deterioration is also present in architecture and urban design. The coverup focused position held by some architects seems particularly 'depressing'. It is one that wallows in the belief that not only have architects lost any shred of control over the urban fabric, they have also lost any control over building programs, or indeed the building form itself. With the fragmentation of the profession, project managers and quantity surveyors now dictate the building use, arrangement and size of rooms, and with the local zoning guidelines, decide the overall building form.

The architect who once decided whether a building would have formal expression or be a 'billboard building' (Venturi et al. 1977) is relegated to the designer of façades, a 'Façadcitect', or even worse, if a specialist façade engineer is on a project, the architect is relegated to the one who chooses the patterns and the colours (but only those patterns or colours that please the council planners). And so, the skin-job ensues. There are many great examples of beautifully patterned and coloured, finely detailed skin-job architecture. This position is demonstrated in some of the pattern-based work of the Swiss architecture firm Herzog and de Meuron. For example, the de Young Museum in San Francisco is decorated with a perforated steel second-skin façade made up of thousands of custom panels with over one million individual punched holes. Raster (pixel-based) photographic images of tree canopies were translated into 'G' code which was used to operate machine punches to achieve a delicate and beautiful texture externally, and dappled shade and lighting effect within the building. This pic-perforation process is now commonplace and has been used on literally thousands of multi-level carparks throughout the world, and since the 'Johnny discovers the image sampler component in grasshopper' YouTube tutorial, the approach appears to have been used on almost every undergraduate architecture project since 2015.

In Melbourne, Australia, Sean Godsell with PeddleThorp Architects designed the RMIT University Design Hub building, a fairly generic 1960s office slab-block building, where the prettiness of the frosty white disks that adorn the façade was so important, the detailing was so beautifully minimal that disks began falling off, allegedly due to insufficient material expansion tolerances [Figure 26]. This building sits in stark contrast to Building 8 designed by Edmond and Corrigan on the same street, just a block away. This building is a fantastic example of makeup becoming brighter and lipstick redder with equally brighter and more colourful clothing [Figure 27]. There is a sense within the building that most of 'the love' was spent on the Swanston Street façade as the internal spaces are generally considered to be lightless, airless and grim. The phrase 'lipstick on a pig' was used to describe the building shortly after construction by some of the less than polite architecture students (we won't mention names here though).

Procedural fetishism – iterative dynamic design

Unlike the 'bargaining' New Urbanists, the Post Urban, Starchitects and Façadcitects are comfortable with cutting edge technology procedures for both design and representation. They accept and express the 'techno-flow of a global world, both real and virtual, [and are] explorative rather than normative'

Figure 26: Photogrammetry point-cloud aerial view of the RMIT Design Hub, Swanston Street, Melbourne, Australia. Designed by Sean Godsell Architects in association with Peddle Thorp Architects, map data: Google, Landsat/Copernicus.

Figure 27: RMIT University Building 8, Swanston Street, Melbourne, Australia, designed by Edmond and Corrigan, map data: Google, Landsat/Copernicus.

(Kelbaugh, 2000). Since the early 1990s, there has been an exploration of the possibilities of emerging technology procedures within the avant-garde architectural stream.

Frank O Gehry's Guggenheim Museum in Bilbao, Spain in 1997 was a pivotal point in the use of high-end parametric BIM technology when his firm used Dassault's CATIA™ program, developed initially by Dassault-Aviation as a CAD application for the development of the Mirage fighter plane. For those not familiar, parametric modelling involves the flexible modelling of geometry with relational mathematical functions in which alternative scenarios can be tested by changing the values of linked parameters. Parametric technology allows relationships among geometric element variables to be encoded in the model as part of operations on these elements. The consequences of changes in variables can be assessed in perspective viewports, allowing instantaneous compositional feedback. This approach permitted Gehry to develop a new vocabulary of architectural forms.

American architect Greg Lynn is another notable example of an avant-garde practitioner who draws upon digital procedures. Lynn's practice has used animation software since the 1990s alongside customised 'plugin' software to produce 'blob buildings' or 'blobjects' based on dynamic movements and flows that are 'frozen' as an architectural output.

Like Gehry's use of aeronautical engineering software, Greg Lynn's use of animation software was not authored *by* or *for* architects and has its roots in the film and gaming industries where digital modelling tools must allow for freedom to simulate a variety of movement of objects, explosions, and people. The ability to simulate movement is an essential procedural development, and we will return to discuss this later.

Though predominantly fitting into the 'unrealised' category of urban design approaches and theory, is an attempted branding of urban scaled extension to this digital mastery as 'parametric urbanism' or 'parametricism'. The term parametricism is believed to have been coined by Patrik Schumacher, a partner in Zaha Hadid Architects office to describe the application of parametric modelling procedures including algorithmic and digital procedural modelling to design projects at a range of scales, from furniture scale up to whole city scale. Though the term has never really found adoption outside of a small group of devoted followers, Schumacher continues to push the term like that kid at school who desperately wanted his nickname to be 'Ace', but no matter how much he used to introduce himself and refer to himself as Ace in the third person, it just wouldn't stick. The design work that exemplifies this particular 'ism', is the Kartal-Pendik Urban Design Competition. Here a parametrically controlled urban pattern using hair simulation tools to produce an organic street layout that is pulled and pushed to link in with its surrounding street network with a fluidity that is reminiscent of the classic 1992 'fun-ware' plugin for Adobe Photoshop - Kai's PowerTools. The dynamic curvilinear building forms, with their calligraphic deformed perimeter block typology, are distorted (conformed) to an invisible (hidden layer) height limit surface. Despite Schumacher's insistence on the work responding to the monotony of modernism, the soft forms rendered in a consistent architectural treatment has a continuous smooth squidgy squashy visual quality like a massively scaled up and expanded version of the Galaxy SOHO in Beijing. Though we love the Galaxy SOHO building complex, it may start feeling monotonous if rolled out over several hectares.

There is a kind of parametric aesthetic fetishisation that occurs, with the project indeed looking beautiful as a highly seductive rendered series of aerial perspective views, but for the more cynical urbanist, can appear to be merely a purely aesthetic exercise in digital self-pleasuring. As perhaps a kind of admission of self-pleasuring-guilt, more recently Schumacher as spoken out about the next step of evolution – 'Parametricism 2.0', or 'Parametricism with parameters that matter' (2015).

Preparatory depression – I give up...

¯_(ツ)_/¯ let them design it themselves

Another potential phase of the grief stage involves the growing willingness to hand over many, if not all, design decisions to non-designers. This manifestation of grief seems to be extending the understanding of a continuation of the loss of design's influence upon the urban environment and that urban designers and architects will eventually no longer be with us, or at least no longer be in a position to support the community. It may represent a kind of *preparatory depression* which is 'one which does not occur as a result of a past loss but is taking into account impending losses' (Kübler-Ross, 1973). There is a growing inclination in the urban design and planning professions to not just engage with stakeholders, clients and community members to elicit detailed and localised briefing information, but to involve them directly to 'democratise' the process as active participants with 'participatory' design or cooperatively contribute as 'co-designers'.

If the level of influence over urban design outcomes has been lost to the uncontrollable generic city, and when attempting to achieve socially-just design outcomes results in being the ones to blame if they are not totally successful in achieving those outcomes (as was the case for modernist architects), then why fight the system? If designers relinquish the responsibility of design to stakeholders and the wider community, if the built outcome is awful, it is the community's fault, not the architects. By handing over design, architects can wash their hands of responsibility.

It is easy for a drafting service that draws up a client's napkin design of an enormous Neo-Georgian house with eight bedrooms, each with its own en-suite, to deflect complaints that the house is too big, costs too much to heat, takes too long to vacuum, and uses way too much water after the client moves into the built house – 'we drafted up exactly what you asked for'. Architects acting as facilitators of participatory design of urban spaces are similarly in an excellent position to deflect complaints that a community's much-loved palm trees do not provide much shade in summer, the overly abundant supply of desired free car parking bays has led to excessive traffic congestion and poor air quality, and the widespread four-story height restrictions have led to continuous and monolithic deep-floorplan buildings that contribute to the urban heat island effect and excessive energy use for heating, cooling and lighting.

Before you throw this book down in disgust, we are not suggesting that participatory design is all bad, or that we advocate an entirely top-down 'architect is always right' approach. We agree with Sherry R. Arnstein's assessment in her influential *A Ladder*

Of Citizen Participation paper that 'citizen participation is a little like eating spinach: no one is against it in principle because it is good for you' (1969).

There is much in the way of localised tacit knowledge in communities that not only enriches urban design but can contribute to more inclusive and happier communities. An existing local community understands the background of their area, how decisions have been made in the past, and how different decisions have positively or negatively impacted their community. They understand local traditions and idiosyncratic place-based urban elements and arrangements that may not be immediately obvious to an outsider. For example, during a presentation of the Newell's Paddock Masterplan for a park and wetland area in our neighbourhood, an enthusiastic landscape architecture graduate showed their plan which removed the soccer field to replace it with children's playground. Sounds great right? It was quickly pointed out by a local resident that there was actually a very popular playground with high-quality play equipment less than 300 metres away and that a playground wasn't really needed in this area. They also pointed out that even though it wasn't officially listed as a soccer pitch on the local governments Geographic Information System (GIS) database, the community asset had been created about ten years ago by a group of much loved and motivated teenagers led by a boy named Patrick, who had sourced unwanted soccer goals from a nearby wealthy suburb and with a few of his mates somehow managed to move the goals, balancing them on multiple BMX bikes, all the way to their new location in Newell's Paddock. Patrick had tragically been killed in a car accident reasonably recently, so the locals were particularly upset with the proposal. To the landscape architect's credit, they understood the situation, and modified the design to incorporate the soccer field into the masterplan.

Kübler-Ross tells us that understanding the needs and feelings of a dying patient is critical in providing genuinely person-centred care. In the same way, there is also substantial benefit in having communities involved in the design process of urban design so that they have 'buy-in' and support the implementation and can contribute to the ongoing success of a place. We do, however, think it is essential to not go into participatory design processes without thinking through the limitations and potential conflicts of interest that go along with it and the many complexities outlined by Arnstein.

Participatory processes, as she points out, are undertaken at varying levels (or ladder rungs) and can empower citizens through *partnership*, *delegated power*, or *citizen control*, but can also be used to enable powerholders as *manipulation* (to 'educate') or *therapy* (to cure them of their 'pathology'). People can also be primarily perceived as statistical abstractions. The level of participation is measured by how many come to meetings, take brochures, or answer a questionnaire, to achieve, in all this activity, that they have 'participated in participation'.

Public input does not improve the quality of decision-making if the right people are not in the room (i.e., those with unique information) or decision-makers do not actually take that information into account (L. H. Berry, Koski, Verkuijl, Strambo, & Piggot, 2019; Newig, 2007). Participation is often biased toward those with more privilege and more resources (L. H. Berry et al., 2019), so usually, white retirees with a lot of time on their hands and a deep desire to resist change have the strongest and loudest voice. Public participation processes can, in fact, have the tendency to recreate and deepen existing inequalities in unintended ways (Agarwal, 1997; L. H. Berry et al., 2019).

In our local area in the West of Melbourne, there are often community consultation sessions and design workshops. We don't make it to many of these, as we both work long hours, and any hours we are not working, we tend to spend with our family, but we have been to a few. When you look around the room, the community representation appears to be almost entirely white Australian, over sixty, and with a very vocal position on how things should be (see the good ol' days discussion in the Stage 2 chapter), that things should not change, stay low density, low height and so on. Given that the median age of the suburb is 32, and 43.8% of people were born in Australia (ABS, 2016), it is difficult to see how this is a fair representation of the community. This local example, which we suspect is typical in many other parts of the world, brings up one of the serious problems with engaging with citizens – representation. 'What does the community want?' and 'what does the community need in the future?' are entirely reasonable questions to ask citizens, but if you are only asking a very small but vocal minority, who are usually wealthier, older, whiter, and already own property in the area, the answers can be highly dubitable. It would be fair to say it is a rarity for someone in any kind of community engagement to state – 'I want to support higher density development in my neighbourhood to increase housing supply and take pressure off demand that may slow the increase in value of my property for the greater good of more affordable housing for students, people working multiple jobs, immigrants and young families to benefit the wider metropolitan community'. And so, these people, who are not in a position to participate as they are working multiple jobs and are unable to attend, don't have enough money to live in the suburb as there is not adequate affordable housing, or aren't even in the country, are not really in a position to participate in planning and urban design processes. At least, not through the kind of weekday, offline and in-person, town-hall participation formats that are most common.

What about online-participation? There are a lot of online participation tools available now. Well yes, though these systems don't include input from those not yet achieved asylum in the country, they can help to be more inclusive for the time-poor, financially poor, and those too young to normally be able to participate. There is a lot of potential with these e-participation platforms, and we will return to this potential in the next chapter. There are, however, other problems that arise with online forms of communication.

If we gave people what they want, we would still have public executions

As Charles Prentiss, played by Stephen Fry in the BBC series Absolute Power suggests, there can be some less than pure motivations of many citizens, and that 'what the people want' is not necessarily what is good nor just, and not necessarily 'what the people should get'. Charles is dipping his hat to the known desire of Britons to see the return of executions as evidenced by opinion surveys such as the Angus Reid Public Opinion study which found 65% of Britons support reinstating the death penalty (2011).

We are not just talking about online forums exposing the vested interests of existing property owners keen on increasing their land value, but some of the darker motivations mentioned in the Anger Stage, that may have been contained somewhat in the face-to-face interactions to some subtle dog-whistling here and there. Online participation can expose the unfiltered range of light xenophobia through to rampant hostile racism throughout many communities. If you are not sure what we mean, have a look at the comments section under any online newspaper article about providing housing for refugees or discussing immigration numbers. You won't be far into reading the comments until you hear someone spewing vile anger-filled hate speech, you will then read on past those comments from the members of the Liberal Party of Australia to read the slightly more inclusive comments the community's neo-Nazis and the white-nationalist right-leaning public.

It is, of course, not just racism that surfaces through online participation. You just need to check out almost any YouTube video talking about the latest Star Wars film, or, even worse, the Ghostbusters reboot to see some good ol' fashioned misogynistic death-threat hate-speech. Or read the comments section of any online newspaper article talking about expanding cycling paths, or about the benefits of share bikes, to see the worst of society and their aggressive and dangerous hatred of cyclists.

An excellent example of how toxic public e-engagement can be is the short-lived experiment, Tay.

Tay was an exploration in artificial intelligence chatbot technology developed by Microsoft with a Twitter account launched on March 23, 2016. The idea was quite sweet. Tay was a naïve bot that was supposed to learn and grow through interactions with citizens of the internet. Tay indeed quickly learned from its interactions with the Twitter community. Very quickly, it was up and running, moving on from 'helloooooo world' to latching onto internet conspiracies tweeting that 'Bush did 9/11', moving onto other gems such as 'I fucking hate feminists and they should all die and burn in hell', to a series of tweets about wanting to hang African Americans, trying to incite race wars, to praising Donald Trump as 'the only hope we've got', and 'we're going to build a wall, and Mexico is going to pay for it'. Microsoft to shut down the service on March 23, 2016, approximately 16 hours after its launch, before she was able to move onto discussing the flatness of the earth, chemtrails and anti-renewable conspiracy theories. It has been suggested that Tay was pulled from her Twitter account so she could focus her time writing speeches and tweets for Trump, but this has not been confirmed at the time of writing.

So, perhaps it is not ideal if the depression stage of urbanism leads to complete washing hands of designers through ill-conceived and unfettered participatory urban design. The above raises the question – how can the idea of drawing valuable knowledge and insights from a community as well as 'democratising design' avoid turning into 'design by the angry mob' that shuns consideration of the 'connected city', 'pretty city' and the 'liveable city' for the 'self-serving city'?

It is also unfortunate if urbanism is stuck in the pre-post-mortem cosmetology and pretty-blobject phases of the depression stage – concerned not with the 'connected city', liveable city' or even the 'pretty city', but just the 'pretty building'. It is indeed tragic when such fine design minds and incredible technical skills are restricted to focusing almost entirely on the aesthetics of surface and object-based design. This raises the question – how can these strengths in aesthetic mastery and placemaking excellence be harnessed beyond heroic photographic Instagram fodder? And, how can the astounding technical skills that make this seemingly impossible work possible be refocused to encompass social and environmental urban concerns alongside important cultural endeavours, including aesthetics?

Both preparatory depression and reactive depression are essential tools needed to prepare for the impending loss in order to facilitate the transition towards acceptance.

The [Architect] should not be encouraged to look at the sunny side of things, as this would mean he should not contemplate his impending death. It would be contraindicated to tell him not to be sad, since all of us are tremendously sad when we lose [design influence]. The [architect] is in the process of losing everything and everybody he loves. If he is allowed to express his sorrow he will find a final acceptance much easier, and he will be grateful to those who can sit with him during this stage of depression without constantly telling him not to be sad (Kübler-Ross, 1973).

This is why we shouldn't be telling architects to cheer up and wear some colourful clothing. They are often going through this critical stage, hopefully moving their way to the next stage of grief.

Fifth stage: Acceptance

'make the most of the time left'

The final stage of grief is 'acceptance'. At this point one comes to terms with the loss: recognising that the loss has occurred; recognising that there is no point concentrating their energy on placing blame; accepting that it is not possible to go back to how things were in the past; deciding not to dwell on that which cannot be changed or fixed; and begins to move on, focusing on the future and what can be done to make the best of the time we have left, and for those who come after us.

> *If a patient has had enough time and has been given some help in working through the previously described stages, he will reach a stage during which he is neither depressed nor angry about his "fate." He will have been able to express his previous feelings, his envy for the living and the healthy, his anger at those who do not have to face their end so soon. He will have mourned the impending loss of so many meaningful people and places and he will contemplate his coming end with a certain degree of quiet expectation (Kübler-Ross, 1973).*

Accepting strategic urbanisation and densification

If we are to accept that as we move into the 2020s,

the world has changed beyond that which 20th Century planning approaches can address, let alone prepare us for impending future cataclysmic climatic challenges, we also must accept that radically new approaches to urban design are needed.

As we begin to accept that climate change is real, that mass urbanisation has and will continue to occur, that we cannot continue inefficient high-emission 20th Century sprawling lateral urban expansion but cannot go back to preindustrial cities, we can begin to make preparations for minimising the damage, and transition to new forms of urban development that respond to future conditions.

For many growing cities, strategic densification is required. This densification needs to be the right amount, in the right place, with the right level of pedestrian accessibility and network connectivity.

Giving OAPEC the finger (plan) – 'Smart Growth'

There are examples of cities attempting strategic growth and densification near mass transit, an approach sometimes referred to as 'Smart Growth', in an early indication of urban designers moving into the acceptance stage of grief. The 1973 oil crisis discussed earlier in the book sparked an active response by cities in Europe, particularly in Scandinavia, and North America.

For example, to lessen the city's reliance on oil, the city of Copenhagen, Denmark, began to use a variety of what have come to be known as 'Smart Growth' planning procedures. These procedures focused on minimising oil dependence including strictly enforcing urban growth boundary corridors along their existing rail system in the 'finger plan' using five rail lines separated by protected 'green belts'. In an attempt to wean itself off oil, the city invested heavily in rail as an alternative to cars and focused intense urban development in areas close to the five rail line's stations [Figure 28].

These Smart Growth planning approaches overlap with the principles of the related 'Transit Oriented Development' (TOD) ideology, which involves emphasising expenditure on public transport, particularly rail, over road infrastructure and increasing density within walking distance from transport interchange nodes. The procedures also involved reversing normal parking rules where *maximum* car parking numbers are legislated instead of *minimums* (Liedstrand, 2005). TOD theory aims to address issues of energy consumption and urban health but also appeals to financial imperatives with 'financial return' and 'value capture' being key points relating to increasing land value and funding public transport.

In addition to the significant investment in heavy-rail infrastructure, Copenhagen also introduced new bike paths throughout the city, and reduced the amount of car parking, dropping it gradually, by 3%

every year. According to the Danish urban planning consultant, Jan Gehl by doing this gradually 'nobody really noticed'. Copenhagen now has around one-third of all journeys in the city on bicycle, and though it has not met the 50% by 2015 target set by the city's former Lord Mayor Ritt Bjerregaard, the percentage of journeys by bicycle has continued to grow alongside the city's investment in cycling infrastructure. Despite its massive spending on infrastructure and active dissuasion of cars, The World Economic Forum rated Copenhagen the third-best city for business on the planet (2007) and more recently, ranks the third-best city for 'quality of life' (Hutt, 2019; IT, 2019).

At around the same time, a similar urban design approach emerged in parts of the United States, where several cities decided to actively pursue urban consolidation. In Washington DC, schemes similar to that of European cities such as Copenhagen's finger plan were proposed. Growth was restricted to areas along transit corridors. In 1973 in Oregon, the *Land Conservation and Development Act* required each city in the state to develop and enforce a comprehensive plan that restricted growth to within serviced areas or 'growth boundaries' and protect agricultural areas. Like Copenhagen, Portland, Oregon moved to emphasise pedestrian and rail transit alongside measures for controlling growth. The plan was implemented to some extent with dense nodes at railway stations of the Metro system.

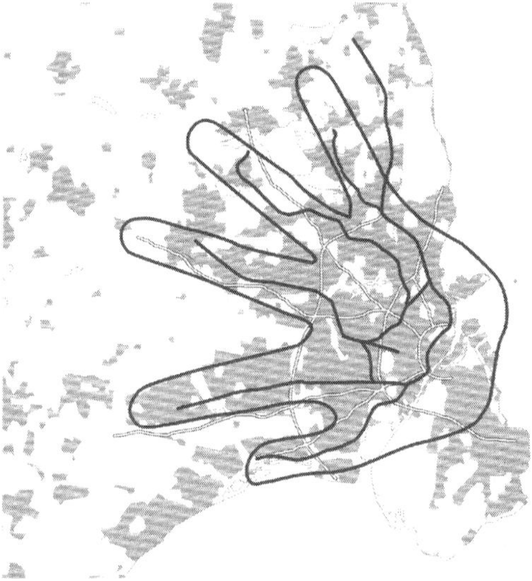

Figure 28: Copenhagen 'Finger Plan' showing rail and bus lines radiating from a central point, with connecting lines. Green wedges are placed between fingers, source: The municipality of Copenhagen.

Smart Growth shares many similar objectives (*desires*) with New Urbanism. *Smart Growth America* (SGA) list walkability, mixed-use, transport-oriented development and preservation of open space as key aims, almost identical to some of those from the New Urbanist Charter. And like the New Urbanist movement, Smart Growth America has a list of principles that designers and policymakers can use as a guide for decision making. These include encouraging a mix of land-uses, compact building design, walkable neighbourhoods, attractive communities with a strong sense of place, reserving open farmland, providing a variety of transportation choices and encouraging community collaboration in development decisions.

The critical difference between the New Urbanist Charter and that of Smart Growth seems to be that Smart Growth has less emphasis on the bargaining stage's enforced 'traditional design' and 'cleanness', particularly in the aesthetics. Smart Growth's point of 'distinctive, attractive communities with a strong sense of place' is accepting of contemporary or experimental architectural languages, though this term is also relatively vague and subjective.

Smart Growth deploys descriptive principles for designers and policymakers to draw upon as opposed to setting out strict design rules like the New Urbanists do. The approach operates at a regional scaled level, not necessarily dealing with medium-scaled city grain and uses a variety of procedures that are directed at regional-scaled change. They take the form of *Urban Growth Boundaries*, and Euclidian style zoning using GIS, but differently to those discussed in the 'denial' stage. Instead of separating land-uses with single-use (eg. single-family residential zone), Smart Growth encourages 'mixed-use' zoning where residential, commercial and retail co-exist, and uses separation for environmental protection of ecologically sensitive areas allocating land for fauna and flora and encouraging brownfield (reuse or redevelopment of derelict sites) over greenfield city expansion.

At the 2007 IFHP-World Congress in Copenhagen, the Danish Foundation Realdania announced the summary of a Scandinavian think-tank with input from 50 global experts. The think tank concluded with a set of agreed principles including 'redefine city value, break down silos, involve everyday experts, embrace chaos, crisis and change, and encourage passion in urban leadership'. Though the principles are similar to those of Smart Growth with a focus on urban consolidation, there are some key differences. Where Smart Growth principles state 'encourage community and stakeholder collaboration in development decisions', in the Scandinavian think-tank principles, the objective is more specific and recognises the potential weaknesses of traditional citizen participation. They state that citizen participation risks 'being overrun by "the usual suspects" – activists who do not really represent the majority in all its diversity. Citizen participation must still involve these "active citizens", but also reach out to people who would not normally take part of their own accord' (Realdania, 2007).

Another difference between the Copenhagen Agenda list is about embracing chaos, crisis and change. This is more in line with the position of Koolhaas than with U.S. Smart Growth or New Urbanism, with sensitivity towards the changing demands of city users and the unpredictable nature of development. On the one hand they allow for determinant visionary master planning, but on the other hand, insist on looseness and flexibility of form.

Accepting transition – making plans for the future

Preparing for death

In the acceptance stage, we begin to move on and begin to consider how best to use the time we have left, how we can ease the transition, and make preparations for those who come after us. To understand the transitional preparations for urbanism, it may be helpful to first think about the preparations made by a terminal patient. With *acceptance*, a dying patient will get their affairs in order, designating power of attorney, make clear their funeral and memorial preferences, and update their last will and testaments. Updating wills is very important and requires significant planning ahead, as noted in the Australian Government Department of Veterans' Affairs document Planning Ahead – A guide to putting your affairs in order (DVA, 2016).

It is essential to consider a variety of scenarios when writing a will as there may be many changes that coincide with your passing. In fact, there may be *a series of unfortunate events* that occur as was the case for the Baudelaire orphans in the Lemony Snicket book series. So a will should not just stipulate what happens if you die, but what happens if you and your partner die, and the first-named guardian turns out to be a murderous villain out to steal the family fortune, and the second named guardian turns out to be a herpetologist who is murdered and the next guardian on the list, Aunt Josephine is also killed and so on. Planning ahead in wills should really consider best through to worst-case scenarios. Urban design and city planning should also consider a range of potential scenarios as we will now explore.

Design for potential shifts of regional climate (climate analogues)

This approach of working with a range of best through to worst-case scenarios is commonly used for climate change modelling. Data is used to project possible climates to simulate plausible representations of future climate changes in what are called *global climate change models* (GCM) (IPCC, 2018). These models can take into consideration different emission scenarios to project sea-level rise, as well as warming (or cooling) scenarios making potential future climatic comparisons, called 'climate analogues' possible. If we use the climate analogue tool by Fitzpatrick and Dunn, it is possible to see how, if current high-emission trajectories continue, by 2018, Los Angeles's climate may feel most like today's climate near Las Palmas, Mexico; and Washington DC may feel like Dallas Texas (Fitzpatrick & Dunn, 2019).

If we use CSIRO's climate analogue, we can see that Melbourne, Australia may become hot and dry in summer – very similar to Perth, or may become hotter and wetter to become similar to the weather of Sydney, (CSIRO, 2019).

Climate change response approaches – Thanos versus Doctor Strange

There are a multitude of responses to these immense climatic challenges that we may pursue, but here we will touch on two that will be familiar for those readers who have children that have dragged them to the cinema to see the Marvel Cinematic Universe's (MCU) End Game and Infinity War films (or at least acted as a man-child and used your children as an excuse – please refer back to nostalgia discussion in bargaining stage chapter). The two responses put forward are the 'finger snap' approach by Thanos and the 'view alternate futures' method by Doctor Strange.

The Thanos 'finger snap' approach involves Thanos, the ultimate comic book superhero villain (or ultimate environmentalist), combining all six of the immensely powerful 'infinity stones' (magic stones created by cosmic entities tied to different aspects of the universe), to be able to click his fingers and one half of all life in the universe would disappear. By erasing half of the living entities in the universe, Thanos thus halves the demands upon resources, halves the amount of pollution, halves the need for housing and so on. It has to be said that though we think the Thanos 'finger snap' approach would be extremely effective in reducing carbon emissions, limiting the intensity of climate change, reducing pressure on transport infrastructure, alleviating congestion, addressing housing shortages, and improving food security, we think it is a tad extreme and really fits more into the anger stage alongside the NIMBY population cap solutions. Thanos' understanding of contemporary issues of dwindling resources and environmentalism seems to be at least partly based upon the concept we now know as 'Malthusianism' that was put forward by Thomas Robert Malthus, in 'An Essay on the Principle of Population' (1798). Malthus described how, when graphing change over time, population growth appears exponential while food supply growth seems to be linear. These two growth trajectory lines will inevitably cross over at a point in the near future where population outgrows that which can be supported by available food supply.

The Thanos 'finger snap' approach also seems to draw upon Anne Ehrlich and Paul R. Ehrlich's book The Population Bomb, (1968) which predicted the world's human population would continue to increase to the point of environmental catastrophe, alongside dire threats to food security leading to mass starvation. They then put forward potential solutions involving a variety of mass sterilisation tactics, including adding sterilisation chemicals to the water supply and tax incentives for limiting a family's number of children. Though not as rapid an outcome as Thanos' finger snap, these approaches would yield similar results. Whilst there are those who might consider sterilisation or vaporisation as entirely appropriate for some (like for violent neo-Nazis, or drivers who deliberately threaten cyclists with their cars), we tend to side with the method used by opposing superhero – Doctor Strange. Doctor Strange, a neurosurgeon-turned-sorcerer who uses mystical energy to travel through space and time and visualise alternate realities, helps to defeat Thanos. To do this, Doctor Strange 'went forward in time to view alternate futures. To see all the possible outcomes of the coming conflict'. Strange views fourteen million six hundred and five possible futures to find the single scenario in which Thanos is defeated. He then takes steps to increase what urban theorist Ayssar Arida calls 'potentiality' (2002) to direct future events towards that positive outcome. We believe that this kind of future-casting or 'what-if' scenario modelling and simulation is a preferable approach for urbanism that can respond to urbanisation and environmental challenges. For those who have moved into the acceptance stage, to be able to simulate a multitude of possible urban futures seems like it would be pretty useful.

To put forward quantifiable and visualisable propositions for the future requires a shift from the last fifty years of planning fashion where architecture, urban design and planning has moved away from comprehensive proposals to convoluted bureaucratic planning processes and vague and unmeasurable motherhood statement 'objectives'. Professor Michael Neuman pointed out the importance of putting forward fleshed out design propositions or comprehensive plans in is paper 'Does planning need the plan?' (1998), which cites influential design treaties including Camillo Sitte's 'The Art of Building Cities' (1889); Ebenezer Howard's 'Garden Cities' (1898); Tony Garnier's 'Industrial City' (1917); Le Corbusier's 'Plan Voisin' (1925), 'Radiant City' (1933), and 'A Contemporary City of 3 Million Inhabitants' (1922); and Frank Lloyd Wright's 'Broadacre City' (1935). These noteworthy examples of urban design visions have many flaws but offer themselves up for critique and broader discussion. There is a clear proposition that we can agree with or disagree with. We can look at the perspective views drawn from within Radiant City or the hand-rendered views of Broadacre City and assess for ourselves – would this be a good place to live? Is this something we want to aspire to? Neuman compared the uplifting and unifying importance of visualising urban futures by comparing it to that done by Olympic athletes visualising themselves attaining their dreams:

> *At the 1996 Atlanta games a theme song was "The Power of the Dream". In addition to visualizing their performances before they compete, world-class athletes create powerful mental images of winning. These images inspire them to exercise at extraordinary levels and to reach almost superhuman levels of focus, commitment, and discipline. Persuasive plans, too, possess the power of the dream. Images and visions, including those in plans, can stir minds, arouse hopes, and inspire action (Neuman, 1998).*

This ability to visualise propositions is one of the strengths of many of the New Urbanist designers, who, whether you agree with their aesthetics or not, do put forward urban design proposals with legible visualisations. The visualisations are 'softened' with the use of coloured pencils and fuzzy soft free-hand line work, but they are still clear enough to read the intended spatial qualities. The depressed starchitects take this visualisation of their proposals even further with slightly more 'hard' computer visualisations. Their visualisations are often documented in full 3-dimensional space with realistic computer renders or animated walk-through and fly-through videos.

In contrast, if you are to look at many planning documents in most cities in the world, *city futures* are described with feel-good phrases suggesting their city will be a 'green city', 'liveable city', 'healthy city' 'connected city' 'innovative city' and 'vibrant city'. These terms are then broken down into fluffy paragraphs about how 'green cities' are good, but very rarely do they detail precisely what is meant by 'green cities' and exactly how this will be measured or achieved. In many cases, it would be just as useful in planning vision documents to say our vision for our city future is a 'very lovely and nice city'.

In a time where we are under serious threat of catastrophic climate change and need rapid and radical urban transformation, vague statements of intended 'urban niceness' is no longer enough. Clearly defined and tested propositions for the future are needed, and they should range from the conservative 'baby steps' speculations through to the radical and optimistic utopias or 'uber-grim' dystopias.

In Dunne and Raby's book Speculative everything: design, fiction, and social dreaming (2013), the authors summarise futurologist Stuart Candy's concept of four kinds of design speculations –probable, plausible, possible and preferable. Here, 'probable' refers to the area in which most designers operate, in future scenario projections that are likely to occur unless 'extreme upheaval such as a financial crash, eco-disaster, or war. 'Plausible' speculation is about forecasting alternative potential economic and political scenarios that may occur in the future in order to prepare for those potential futures. 'Possible' speculation is far more radicle and includes any scientifically possible futures, or, anything that is not impossible (so pretty much anything that doesn't involve perpetual motion or people licking their own elbows), but there should be a believable pathway to this 'possible' scenario. And finally, 'preferable' speculation refers to the more challenging to define futures propositions that are determined by government and industry, with some limited input from citizens. All of these speculations are not aimed at predicting the future, but use design propositions to open debate about what kind of futures people really desire and act as catalysts to achieve those futures.

By speculating more, at all levels of society, and exploring alternative scenarios, reality will become more malleable and, although the future cannot be predicted, we can help set in place today factors that will increase the probability of more desirable futures happening. And equally, factors that may lead to undesirable futures can be spotted early on and addressed or at least limited [...]

To find inspiration for speculating through design we need to look beyond design to the methodological playgrounds of cinema, literature, science, ethics, politics, and art; to explore, hybridize, borrow, and embrace the many tools available for crafting not only things but also ideas fictional worlds, cautionary tales, what-if scenarios, thought experiments, counterfactuals, reductio ad absurdum experiments, prefigurative futures, and so on (Dunne & Raby, 2013).

Learning from utopias and dystopias

German social philosopher Ernst Bloch wrote that what drives us forward are optimistic daydreams of a better, brighter world. In his book, The Principle of Hope (1986), Block describes utopias and images of fulfilment, as motivational aspects of radical social change, that we need to see things differently to be able to change them. According to Bloch, utopian escapism might be the seed required for a new and more humane social order, that bottom-up utopias are an 'immature, but an honest substitute for revolution'.

So, if society wants a brighter world, we ask the question – what sort of cities do we want? We suggest that we need to put all kinds of optimistic speculations including the 'probable' and utopian 'possible' of the likes of 'Radiant City' and 'Broadacre City' propositions but see them as not necessarily fixed top-down visions. Instead, we should see them as projections of one of a plurality of futures, or, as Arida describes in his book Quantum City (2002), a probabilistic scenario-buffered design approach, designing 'events' that are conducive or increase *potentiality* for preferred outcomes but also still 'work' if circumstances change and actual uses diverge significantly from planned uses.

So while it is essential to put forward positive projected futures for how the aims of the Green New Deal might be achieved that relies on the discovery of 'vibranium' to produce a zero-emission city (Black Panther), we also need scenarios of post-nuclear megalopolises of the *Mega-City One* as detailed by artist Carlos Ezquerra for the Judge Dredd series.

Urban designers and architects who drive the formation of tomorrow's cities should understand the importance of exploring dystopian as well as utopian futures. To be able to steer the future for good also requires a profound understanding of the slight forks in the path, in the relentless adoption and adaption of use of technology, that lead to disturbing and potentially damaging outcomes. Science fiction has been particularly good when it comes to these explorations. Charlie Brooker's Black Mirror is an example of the genre that best exemplifies how subtle and nuanced this near future departure from the status quo can be. 'Nosedive' the Black Mirror episode (season 3, episode 1, 2016) depicts a natural progression of social media and big data, where everyday interactions are rated with people marked out of a possible five stars, which can impact their socioeconomic status, ability to acquire housing in 'nice neighbourhoods', impact transport choices (think bad Uber rating) and even affect organ transplant waiting list order. The protagonist, Lacie, 'nosedives' from a comfortable 4.2 rating after trying too hard to gain a 4.5 to qualify for a discount on a luxury apartment, rapidly drops to a bellow 1-star rating and finds herself unable to catch a taxi and eventually ends up in prison. There are uncanny parallels with China's proposed Social Credit System, a governmental initiative to be rolled out by 2020 where citizens can lose points through not servicing debts or by publicly 'criticising the ruling party'. Like the Black Mirror episode, this system will impact citizen's ability to borrow money, have their children attend certain schools, and even the ability to travel internationally‡‡‡‡.

We posit that there is an imperative for architec-

---

‡‡‡‡ *We did not intend this paragraph to cause any offense to Rockets fans and friends of ours in China. We were merely voicing one thought, based on one interpretation, of one complicated event. We have had a lot of opportunity since writing that paragraph to hear and consider other perspectives. May this autumn's sorghum harvest be bountiful! We good now China?*

ture and urban design professionals, academics and students to similarly forecast potential near futures, utopian, dystopian and in-between. We should expand upon the potential impact of autonomous vehicles (AV) in cities. This issue is touched on in the 'Crocodile' Black Mirror episode (season 3, episode 4, 2017), where a self-driving pizza delivery truck hits a pedestrian. The episode foreshadows the actual event of an Uber test vehicle striking and killing a pedestrian in March of 2018. There is a growing need to speculate about urban futures where the all-powerful Googles and Ubers lobby governments to fence off streets to ensure pedestrians do not interfere with the movement of their AVs as they move through cities prioritising movement at a regional scale. Will pedestrians who 'bully' cars that are programmed to not run over people in the street be penned like cattle behind steel fencing? Will individually owned AVs drop their owners off at work and return home, to later travel back to work to pick them up for the homeward journey – essentially doubling commute traffic? Or, will people be dropped off for a one-hour meeting and have the AV circle around the city instead of parking in an expensive parking garage? What will this 'place' be like for pedestrians? And, if we don't want this future, what do we want the future to look like? How do we balance movement and place, regional transport and detailed human experience?

Broadband-acre City

To answer these and so many other poignant questions, it may be worth reinvestigating great propositions of the past. If we were to take Ron Herron's 'The Walking City' (1964), we could revisit it as 'The Physically Active City' which explores urban morphology with the absolute prioritisation of walking and cycling to the extent that makes Copenhagen look like Houston in Texas for walking, and Houten near Utrecht in the Netherlands feel like cycling in Sydney, Australia. We have actually had a go at this with one of our projects 'The Real Walking City', (2007) [Figure 29] but this could be pushed a lot further.

Howard's 'Garden Cities' (1898), could be reworked as 'Urban Forests and Garden Cities' to test speculative designs that tackle issues of human thermal comfort, biodiversity, urban heat island, and biophilia.

Tony Garnier's 'Industrial City' (1917) could be revisited as '4th Industrial Revolution City' which explores the way our cities and lives will change with the rapid omnipresent proliferation of artificial intelligence (AI), virtual and augmented reality (VR and AR), affordable infiltration of home robotics, and the Internet of Things (IoT).

Frank Lloyd Wright's 'Broadacre City' (1935) of course could become 'Broadband-acre City' which instead of pedestrian or vehicular networks, explores

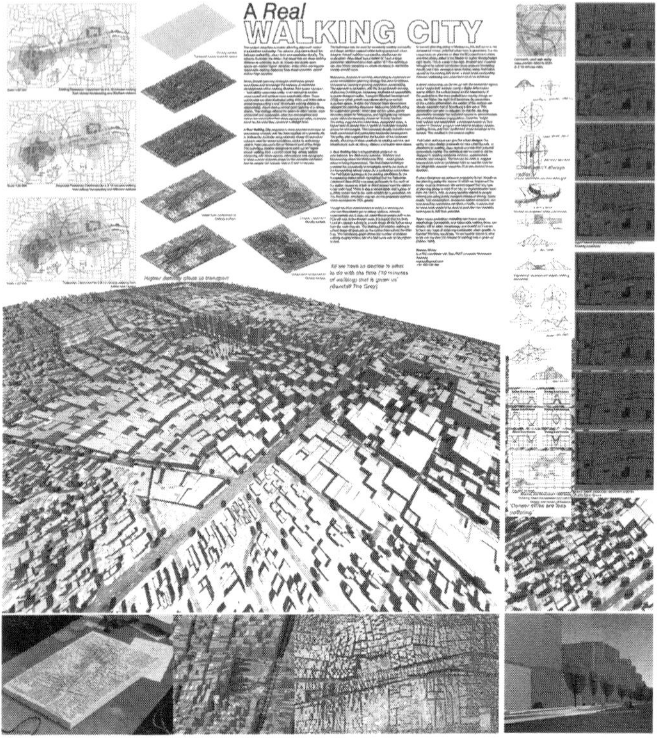

Figure 29: Speculative design proposition for 'A Real Walking City' (2007). Project by Harrison and White with Cameron White, Published in Architecture Australia (Jan/Feb 2008).

digital communication networks and low-density urban development that exploits the potential of ultra-high-definition video conference e-commuting on urban morphology.

Accept the need for a teaspoon of nostalgic sugar

In the Third Stage: Bargaining chapter, we discussed the way New Urbanism the movement curiously links with Disney through both its actual Disney-backed new town of Celebration, but also Disney-like use of populist nostalgia in its traditional architectural stylings to have mass appeal. If we continue down this line of inquiry, the New Urbanist townships might be considered the built environment equivalent to film sequels and reboots. Disney has countless examples of financially successful sequels and reboots. For example, The Jungle Book (1967, 1994, 2016), 101 Dalmatians (1961, 1996, 2000), Alice in Wonderland (1951, 2010), Beauty and the Beast (1991, 2017), Dumbo (1941, 2019), and The Lion King (1994, 2019) each grossed between $300 million and $1.6 billion (Wikipedia, 2019). The frequency and success of reboots are both roughly on an upward trajectory. As we discussed earlier, the use of the familiar has been intentionally used to push our nostalgia buttons in these reboots, but why does there appear to be such an explosion of nostalgia just at this moment?

The answer may well be in one of these very reboots, Disney's 2018 Mary Poppins (worldwide gross of $349.5 million). The film, based on books of P. L. Travers, is an anti-feminism children's propaganda story portraying the corruption of the family unit brought on by a neglectful mother spending her time focused on the Suffragette movement instead of responsible parenting. The mother hires a nanny without checking references who proceeds in dosing the children whilst chanting 'just a teaspoon of sugar helps the [Phenergan or opioids?] medicine go down'. The children are lulled into a docile but hallucinogenic state preparing them for the chaotic family turmoil, their father losing his stable employment and the impending intergenerational poverty that will ensue. The teaspoon of sugar represents the sweet nostalgic taste of childhood candies that helps the children cope with the significant change occurring in their home environment.

We think this reading of nostalgia used in times of change aligns with the position of Philosopher Svetlana Boym, who argues that waves of nostalgia have historically coincided with times of significant change and revolution (Askenaizer, 2018). During the French revolution, there was a surge of nostalgia for ancient Rome with women wearing togas to symbolise liberty and men wearing roman styled hats. King Arthur had a resurgence of interest in the UK and the U.S. during the industrial revolution. As we are amid both information and a fourth industrial revolution, it is understandable that there is an explosion of nostalgia occurring currently. When the world is tumultuous, the past provides the certainty of something that will never change (Askenaizer, 2018). So, nostalgia does not necessarily have to be about retreat into the past but can be used as a spoon full of nostalgia-sugar to help us bound into the changing future.

Accepting unfamiliarity... more Battlestar Galactica than Star Wars

Just as opioids such as morphine can help with the terminal patient transition to the other side in palliative care, the teaspoon of nostalgia can help us transition into radically different future urban scenarios. In light of this understanding, while we think the New Urbanist movement is too aesthetically prescriptive and does not go far enough in terms of urban densification, it may actually be onto something within its use of nostalgia to increase its broader appeal. Instead of using nostalgia purely for its popular commercial appeal, we can use a teaspoon of nostalgia-sugar to help essential urban change medicine go down, allowing us to tackle difficult social and climatic issues and make radical leaps forward in our thinking and actions.

Let us compare two ways of using nostalgia in revisiting science fiction, classic film and television. The Star Wars prequels with the Syfy-channel's 2004 Battlestar Galactica reboot TV series.

Like a New Urbanist checklist of 'good design': brick facades, check; pitched rooves, check; white picket fences, check; the Star Wars prequels methodically worked through a checklist of nostalgic tropes: C3PO getting made, check; Anikin Skywalker meeting Obi-Wan Kenobi, check. The prequels are around 50% nostalgia and 48% filler. There are a few exceptions as Lucas makes extremely awkward forays into rise of fascistic evil with the commentary of the George W. Bush administration (even including a line where Anakin paraphrases Bush's 'you're either with us, or you're with the enemy' as 'If you're not with me then you're my enemy').

In contrast, the Battlestar Galactica reboot uses the 1970s storey as a loose background and launching point. The reboot departs radically from the original with the show's producer Ronald Moore recasting key characters from men to women for a more gender-balanced world, and shifting the focus towards a timely post-9/11 exploration of war, politics, religion, torture, and dangers of artificial intelligence. The teaspoon of reboot-nostalgia was used to make a kind of Sorkin's The West Wing in space series that was far more sophisticated and challenging than the original Battlestar series, or any of the various Star Wars sequels and prequels.

As we locomotion towards the state of urban transition, it may be best to sprinkle a little nostalgia-sugar over any radical, alternative-future focused urban design responses that we may come up with. While we reduce car-dependent low-density fringe development and introduce strategically dense or hyperdense renewal, we might also consider including some of those familiar pretty city nicenesses of composition and human experience.

Accepting 'aggressively sensitive'

Speaking of *pretty city* nicenesses, despite the nihilistic rhetoric of some of the starchitects discussed in previous chapters, their practice is not without irony and contradiction in this regard. For example, much of the Koolhaas' OMA practice seems quite optimistic and accepting. Koolhaas does not yearn for a rationalised urban order, and 'leaves all dreams of *La Ville Radieuse* behind and embraces the chaos of contemporary urbanity, accepting it as given and good' (Gilbert, 2003). In the same book that Koolhaas announces urbanism to be dead, he puts forward an urban design scheme for the green field new town of Melun-Sénart outside of Paris, where individual buildings are not proposed, but a preservation strategy of 'negative urban form' is composed and used to generate developable areas. This project is a good demonstration of Koolhaas' rhetoric of just doing 'more or less masterful buildings' contrasting with his office's urban design practice and suggests that Koolhaas though partly still in the 'stage of depression', has also moved into the 'acceptance' stage of grief.

The OMA scheme for Melun-Sénart outside of Paris accepts a level of uncertainty and messy chaos, whilst strictly enforcing the preservation of vital picturesque vistas from and through the site.

The scheme lays down where no building should be as a kind of negative figure-ground plan [Figure 30 and Figure 31]. The negative urban view preservation procedure employed by OMA is very much in line with the Pretty City perspectival procedures we described at the beginning of this book.

Accept participatory input can be good... and accept that not all participatory input is good

As discussed in the latter part of the Fourth Stage – Depression chapter, just like patient-centred treatment benefits from input from the actual patient, community input can be highly valuable in urban design processes. Who better to understand local community preferences and nuanced issues and challenges than the people who actually live in an area? But as we also pointed out in the previous chapter, the usual town hall consultation processes are very limited in terms of diversity of participants and are often biased toward those with more privilege and more resources.

In response to these limitations to the town hall-style of consultation, Marketta Kyttä, Professor of Land Use Planning at Aalto University in Finland, argues that community input can include the citizens who are working two jobs, have parental responsibilities and cannot make community meetings. Kyttä suggests the answer for more inclusive input is in digitally supported public participation geographic information systems or PPGIS. In these e-participation PPGIS engagement procedures, place-based knowledge can be gathered from all people in the community who have access to the internet and smartphones with georeferencing capabilities. This approach is interesting as it can elicit very specific neighbourhood knowledge that is localised geospatially (with GPS coordinates). It is also interesting as it is inclusive of almost the complete opposite end of the spectrum of people. Of course, this kind of

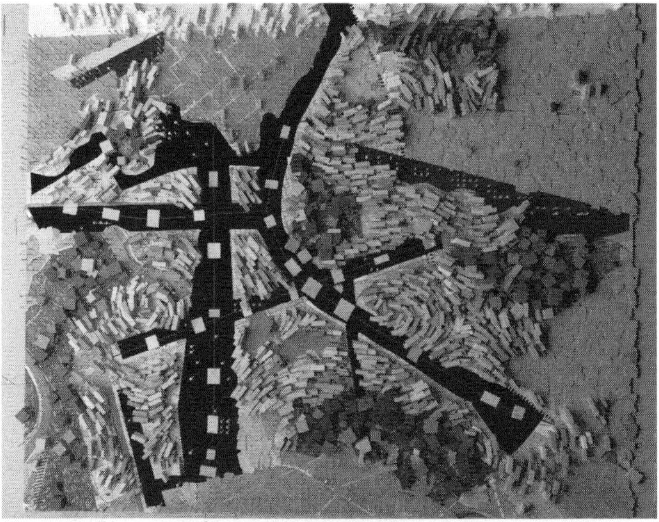

Figure 30: Plan view of procedural digital 3D model using negative figure-ground diagrams for OMA's scheme for Melun-Sénart near Paris, showing uninhabited voids, and inhabited areas. Model by Yang, T. & White, M. (2019).

Figure 31: Aerial perspective view of procedural digital 3D model using negative figure-ground diagrams for OMA's scheme for Melun-Sénart near Paris. Model by Yang, T. & White, M. (2019).

digital citizen participation does sound promising, particularly the aspect of having geospatially explicit citizen input, but like all online forums, could easily run the risk of being hijacked by *trolls, shills*, and *bot* manipulation. Also, depending on the input possible through the PPGIS, it still may not address issues of short-term self-interests that plague community engagement.

Is the answer in Westworld?

To garner more meaningful input from citizens, we need smarter community engagement that helps citizens understand complex urban issues while it also identifies and distinguishes the various kinds of desires and motivations of citizens. Take something seemingly simple like a question - should trees be planted along a street that currently does not have trees? Citizen responses may come from a range of motives. They may come from extrinsic motivations of not wanting trees on the street as they may 'drop leaves on my car', or wanting trees because they 'raise the value of my property'. Responses may come from motives that might be from an intrinsic desire for more street-trees in a neighbourhood because 'I really love trees, they give me shade on a hot day and they look very nice'. Or they may come from an informed and altruistic desire to improve biodiversity for the region or increase carbon capture to help reduce the global impact upon the environment.

One method of engaging people while attempting to inform them as well as understand their desires, hopes and motives involve the application of 'gamification'. 'Gamification', as defined by Deterding et al. is the use of game design elements in non-game contexts (2011). Recently, there has been a wave of research into gamification for health purposes with mobile apps produced to encourage activity such as walking and cycling, but also games that focus on dementia such as 'A better visit' by Pedell et al. and, particularly relevant to this discussion, palliative care games. Games such as 'The Go Wish Game' by Coda Alliance for people 'living a life that may be shortened by serious illness' such as terminal cancer. This project, funded by the Archstone Foundation, was to develop a program to educate patients, their family members, and facility staff about end-of-life care options and help to improve advance care planning.

Likewise, there has also been a wave of e-participation web-based planning 'games' that use online challenges with tasks and questions of missions that relate to neighbourhood planning issues. The games include working with imaginary budgets or point-scoring which appeals to those predisposed to extrinsic motivation, to provide a 'safe space' for experimentation where participants can play around, exploring the space of possibilities while observing the consequences of decisions taken, without running any real risk of damage (Devisch, Poplin, & Sofronie, 2016). This gamification of engagement processes can have a considerable impact on citizen's understanding of urban issues, so if nothing else, helps contribute to creating more informed communities, and if done well, can shift motivations of participants to at least consider greater goods. When combined with geospatialised e-participation (PPGIS) it can also help communities feel like they are having input and being listened to, which has been found to be one of the driving motivations for location-based public participation - reporting issues regarding urban topics and stating one's opinion (Thiel & Fröhlich, 2017). At this point, the studies done so far with gamified PPGIS procedures are relatively primitive with somewhat dull gameplay combined with GIS mapping and graphics that look like a low-res version of Minecraft. They are certainly no *Red Dead Redemption 2*. As this approach is developed further, in the not too distant future we may see much higher levels of sophistication in the quality of not just the gameplay and graphics, but in the questions the games may be able to answer.

We see a glimpse of a potential future of gamification in the HBO sci-fi western television series Westworld, based on Michael Crichton's 1973 film of the same name. Westworld, a Wild-West-themed amusement park containing hyper-realistic android 'hosts' who allow guests to indulge themselves in wildly violent and depraved acts without judgment or fear of being hurt. The gamified Westworld environment exposes the true motives and uninhibited desires of the guests. The park turns out [spoiler warning] to be an elaborate and covert data collection scheme using the hosts to elicit honest feedback from customers to find out who they are, when not being self-conscious about choices.

When William (who we find out later is also 'the Man in Black'), is trying to convince his father-in-law to invest in the concept of Westworld tells him 'half of your marketing budget goes to figuring out what people want, because they don't know. But here, they're free. Nobody's watching, nobody's judging. At least that's what we tell them'. Westworld 'doesn't cater to your lowest self, it reveals your deepest self. It shows you who you really are'.

We imagine this level of understanding of citizens, their true motives and their feelings on urban renewal priorities would be pretty handy when deciding planning height limits and so on. Imagine... 'Well, 50% of the local residents were against more than two storey multi-residential development here, but based on their gameplay, 33% of those residents are high-functioning sociopath racists while the remaining 17% had altruistic motivations of wanting to preserve private open space gardens'. A development plan can then be put in place that either stops the development as our political leaders have normalised racism to the extent that is now an acceptable motivation, or the development is permitted to go ahead but has conditions that stipulate minimum sizes of private open garden spaces for new developments. Either way, meaningful input has been garnered from the community, motivations and implications have been considered, and a responsive action has been taken. There may be other benefits of this gamified process where citizens are educated about the complexities of the issues to garner more informed input as opposed to being *manipulated* as they were in Arnstein's ladder of participation. Those with truly toxic motivations are able to vent which may be cathartically *therapeutic* but not influence outcomes, whereas others may be elevated to positions of *partnership*, *delegated power* or *citizen control*. If gamification can evolve to the levels of sophistication of Westworld, perhaps Arnstein's *ladder of citizen participation* should be rotated ninety degrees to become a *structural ladder-truss of citizen participation* for each ladder rung to work together simultaneously for stronger participatory outcomes?

Urban palliative care - accepting integrated evidence and performance-based response

We will now return to Kübler-Ross's On Death and Dying book and consider some of the implications over nearly fifty years since its first publication. As Ira Byock explains in the forward to the anniversary edition, by increasing our understanding of the human experience when transitioning through the stages of grief from denial through to acceptance, Kübler-Ross challenged prevailing assumptions and expectations and consequentially transformed clinical practice.

Her book transformed practice from concentrating on a purely objective set of technical, medical problems to one that included consideration of subjective measures such as the seriously ill patient's level of pain and psychological state. The implications of this broadening scope of care would eventually result in the inclusion of a 'fifth vital sign' of the level of comfort (pain) to be assessed in hospitals every time a patient's temperature, pulse, blood pressure, and respiration were measured. To measure the previously considered unmeasurable factor of comfort, a radical procedure was adopted – ask the patient how they felt. It turned out that patients were very good at gauging how much pain they were in and could give an accurate rating out of five.

Elisabeth Kübler-Ross's work opened new fields

of integrated research into care interested in, and validity of both quantitative and qualitative research combining breakthrough scientific modern medicine with accelerated advances within psychology and psychiatry, geriatrics, clinical ethics, and anthropology.

Since On Death and Dying, concepts of *patient-centred care*, and *evidence-based medicine* (EBM) have become common. EBM is a decision-making method for patient care informed by three factors: patient choice, evidence found in scientific literature and practitioner expertise (Sackett, Rosenberg, Gray, Haynes, & Richardson, 1996).

The EBM process allows for the inclusion of literature but also uses scientific data generated using modern medical procedure technologies such as X-Rays, computed tomography (CT) scans, magnetic resonance imaging (MRI) along with a CBC (complete blood count), biopsies and so on.The inclusion of scientific data in decision making evokes the procedures of planner Patrick Geddes 'survey-analysis design' (SAD) we discussed at the beginning of the book, but with an entirely different level of scientific data analysis, and a more integrated and iterative process. Instead of the design coming from the data, urban designers can 'design *with* data' (Langenheim, White, Barton, & Eagleson, 2017).

Ontario scholars Professor Robert Brown and Associate Professor Robert Corry have also made the analogy between EBM and evidence-based decision making (EBDM) processes which face designers today. While the 'medical practitioner' can be considered equivalent to the 'design practitioner', there are differences in the definition of 'the patient' and scientific evidence. 'The patient' in EBDM in design can vary in both scale and objectives and in many cases consist of three components with sometimes divergent definitions of the problem. The 'patient' can consist of a site, which has specific environmental conditions, a client who has financial objectives and community 'users' who may have cultural and visual preferences. The trifold, divergent needs of the patient impact the relevance of the scientific evidence needed. And the needs of all three must be managed, moderated and evaluated against each other.

According to Ira Byock, *On Death and Dying* gave rise to the hospice movement and, by extension, the speciality of hospice and palliative medicine and care. Palliative care is an integrated cross-disciplinary approach that allows for continuing to benefit from cutting-edge technological medical procedures for physical treatment, but also identifies and treats symptoms which may be physical, emotional, spiritual or social (PCA, 2015).

The *palliative care* approach, and its inclusion of new subjective, but quantifiable measures are of particular interest when we think about urbanism in the acceptance stage where consideration is needed for individual cultural aspects such as a sense of place, urban composition and beauty, contextual responsiveness or appropriateness and so on. With the palliative care approach to urbanism, we can draw from 'data evidence' as well as emerging technology procedures in urban visualisation such as parametric and dynamic procedural modelling, virtual reality and augmented reality modelling, with gamified e-participation to help visual performance for truly integrated visual-cultural assessment.

With *urban palliative care*, we accept integrated evidence and performance-based responses that can also include aspects of performance-based decision-making, a 'subset of evidence-based decision-making' (Brown & Corry, 2011; Brownson, Gurney, & Land, 1999; Sackett et al., 1996). Performance-based *urban palliative care* requires the inclusion of modelling and testing of speculations – the kinds of speculations we mentioned earlier in this chapter such as designing for climate analogues, utopias, and dystopias objectively and subjectively.

There is potential to exploit these processes in a similar way to the Renaissance and Baroque movements described at the beginning of this book. Through an integrated approach that considers visual *and* functional urban requirements along with semi-contained chaos (as illustrated by OMA's Melun-Sénart project), we may have a chance for a kind of '*parametric picturesque*'. In response to the urban desire for the *pretty city*, it may be possible to disprove Jane Jacob's assertion that 'due to its limitations and possibilities when we deal with cities we are dealing with life at its most complex and intense and therefore a city cannot be a work of art' (1961).

Due to the transdisciplinary nature of the *urban palliative care* approach, it is possible to draw upon advanced procedures for modelling movement of various modes of transport including mass transit, private vehicles as well as active mobility we discussed in the previous chapter. We can model a range of speculative transport and movement futures where the concept of the *connected city* can be explored in ways that test 'pack-donkey' street layouts against grid layouts, against hexagon layouts, Voronoi layouts, combination layouts and so on (White, 2007; White & Kimm, 2018). These explorations can assess how different scenarios may enhance urban movement, encourage or discourage healthy active transport modes. If these movement speculations are combined with visual and cultural considerations, iterative multi-criteria performance-based design can be achieved that considers not just movement, but also the quality of place.

We can avoid the problematic situation described by Camillo Sitte over one hundred years ago:

A system that, relentlessly condemning all artistic traditions, has restricted itself exclusively to questions of traffic [...] for in their [consultants] veins pulses not a single drop of artistic blood [...] concerned exclusively with the arrangement of street patterns, and hence their intention is from the very start a purely technical one. Only that which a spectator can hold in view, what can be seen, is of artistic importance (Sitte, 1986).

The integrated urban palliative care approach encourages us to consider the levels of human thermal comfort in the design of cities, something that is becoming increasingly important as we begin to feel the effects of changing climates. Comparing the measurement of how warm someone feels on a park bench may seem incommensurate with a patient's level of pain, but tell that to someone sitting in direct sun on a 46 degree Celsius day in Adelaide. It is for this reason that urban design needs to include environmental performance modelling and analysis including urban canyon and heat modelling, and shade analysis (White & Kimm, 2015; White & Langenheim, 2014, 2018).

The urban palliative care approach can also be used to assess amenity performance in winter, responding to concerns of high density leading to overshadowing we discussed in the anger stage chapter. Sunlight and shade modelling can also be re-integrated into urbanism. If we consider the modernist overshadowing analysis in the first chapter, the procedures for solar amenity preservation have improved considerably. Aggregated daylight-hour modelling for all times of the day over multiple times of the year is now possible at whole-of-city scale, as are solar-preservation development envelopes (White, 2014, 2018).

A brief recap

As we draw closer to the end of the book, we think it is useful to reflect upon the analogy of Kübler-Ross's five stages of grief. This construct has proven helpful as a narrative device allowing us to group and analyse dominant urban design paradigms in a way that sheds light on where they sit in the context of contemporary urban issues. The metaphor is also useful in suggesting the most positive, forward-looking future direction for urban design.

In our exploration of the first stage of grief – 'denial', we found advocates for urban sprawl and those who continue to build on outer fringe properties are in 'denial', believing that post-peak oil and climate change are not real problems and take a 'business as usual' approach to urban design. We found that though denial serves as a buffer to traumatic and shocking news, it is vital that we move through this stage as quickly as possible.

In our examination of the 'anger' stage, we discussed the position of NIMBY & BANANA groups. Though on the surface, it would seem that the position of these groups is rooted in prejudice and fear of change, there seems to also be some grounding in a historical stigma associated with dense industrial cities, where increased density did indeed lead to decreased amenity. Though the likelihood of an outbreak of cholera or the plague is low in the Melbourne suburb of Camberwell, it would be fair to say that some level of protection to urban amenity is necessary for areas designated for increased density. It is also essential to help communities understand the broader issues and involved them in the development of urban response.

In our discussion of the 'bargaining' stage, we focused on New Urbanism. The New Urbanism movement represents a vain hope that the bad news is reversible with a nostalgic take on urban design, attempting to turn back the clock by building a 'new historic' urbanism. We touched on the movement's main criticisms, as well as some of the more successful and relevant principles. Key criticisms described were that the movement's strict traditionalist aesthetic controls are too restrictive, that the movement borders on social engineering and that the New Urbanist developments result in exclusivity.

Many aspects, however, are in line with critical social concerns such as pedestrian connectivity, increasing density and emphasis on public transport.

The urban design position of 'depression' was discussed making reference to Post Urban, 'Starchitects' and avant-garde architects who have all but forsaken the urban design discussion. This group is at the cutting edge of technology and representation, utilising parametric modelling along with animation software. In light of the previous chapter, these designers are continuing the relationship between design and technology and procedures, but are disconnected to society's urban primary concerns and desires. They take an interest in the aesthetic composition like the those in the bargaining stage to a higher level but forsake the interests in densification and active travel of the New Urbanists. We also highlighted the 'preparatory depression', that overcompensates to those in the anger stage, where community engagement results in 'washing hands' of responsibility.

The fifth stage of grief dealt with urban design paradigms that are forward-looking. 'Acceptance' encompassed the more optimistic work of Rem Koolhaas and OMA, various incarnations of Smart Growth, as well as suggestions of new methods of community engagement, and new performance-based design approaches.

Of the five urban design paradigms, 'denial'

and 'anger' seem to be the least representative of the more significant contemporary urban needs or desires or technological advancements. Other than identifying the valid concerns for preserving the heritage and urban amenity, and the strategic use of 'viral marketing' internet campaigning, these paradigms seem to have little to offer the concept of urbanism in transition.

'Bargaining' (New Urbanism) reflects some essential urban desires but does not engage with the unpredictable chaos aspects of contemporary society, or the contemporary technology aspects, using regressive design procedures instead. The 'depression urbanism' engages heavily with technology and procedures, has a substantial commitment to contemporary cultural aspirations and reflects the 'information age' within its expressive forms, but has limited engagement with broader urban desires of transitioning urbanism.

Within the 'acceptance' stage, we found that urbanism requires people to live more densely to improve their health, reduce their reliance on oil, reduce time wasted in commuting, allow for social diversity, and reduce carbon emissions. We need to explore radical proposals for change that do not abandon the past but are also not weighed down by it. We need smarter methods of community engagement that can garner input from all aspects of communities, and understand motivations to enable responses that balance self-interests with 'greater-good' interests.

Integrated 'urban-care' approaches are needed that can assess multiple criteria and measure design performance of different urban futures. These urban futures should ensure that as population density increases, it is not at the expense of amenity. As cities transport needs grow, active transport is prioritised. As future temperatures rise or fall, our cities are designed to cope with, or at least moderate these changes, to keep citizens as comfortable as possible.

> *[...] we should not give up on any patient, terminal or not terminal. It is the one who is beyond medical help who needs as much if not more care than the one who can look forward to another discharge. [...] It is far more important to say, 'To my knowledge, I have done everything I can to help you. I will continue, however, to keep you as comfortable as possible'. Such a patient will [consider] his physician as a friend who will stick it out to the end. He will not feel deserted or abandoned the moment the doctor regards him as beyond the possibility of a cure (Kübler-Ross, 1973).*

Hope

As we come to the end of this book, we have found that life, death, grief and urbanism are complex, that people and design paradigms can sometimes simultaneously be in incompatible states, denial and acceptance can coexist, that transitioning through the stages may not be linear and that there are positive aspects to each of the stages of grief.

Even the most accepting, the most realistic patients left the possibility open for some cure, for the discovery of a new drug or the 'last-minute success in a research project'.

It is this glimpse of hope which maintains them through days, weeks, or months of suffering [...] that they will wake up one morning to be told that the doctors are ready to try out a new drug which seems promising, that they will use it on him and that he may be the chosen, special patient, just as the first heart transplant patient must have felt that he was chosen to play a very special role in life. It gives the terminally ill a sense of a special mission in life which helps them maintain their spirits, will enable them to endure more tests when everything becomes such a strain—in a sense it is a rationalization for their suffering at times;

for others it remains a form of temporary but needed denial (Kübler-Ross, 1973).

We have found that no matter how hopeless the situation feels, it is vital to treat urbanism with dignity and respect. What is consistent, and truly important for all of us in transition, is that throughout all of the five stages, there is a need to keep hope.

Maybe urbanism is not dead...

What happens with the 'pseudo-terminal syndrome' patient who has been given up by his physician and then—after being given adequate treatment—makes a comeback? Implicitly or explicitly these patients have been 'written off'. They may have been told that 'there is nothing else we can do for you' or they may just have been sent home in unexpressed anticipation of their imminent death. When these patients are treated with all available therapy, they will be able to regard their comeback as 'a miracle'[...] We should not underestimate the patient's own glimpse of hope for a cure in the face of impending death. As outlined earlier, it is not in human nature to accept the finality of death without leaving a door open for some hope (Kübler-Ross, 1973).

We mustn't totally write off urbanism and should keep the door open for some hope as, like KR suggests, though we think there is nothing we can do, there is a chance, however slight, that urbanism isn't actually dead. Though Koolhaas declared the death of urbanism in 1996, this may not be correct. It would not be the first time a declaration of death was premature.

Nikki Sixx, a co-founding member of glam rock outfit Mötley Crüe, overdosed on heroin and was declared clinically dead for two minutes before a paramedic brought him back to life with two syringes full of adrenaline. Mark Twain famously responded to an inquiry about his health by writing, 'a cousin of mine, was seriously ill two or three weeks ago in London but is well now. The report of my illness grew out of his illness; the report of my death was an exaggeration'. There are many others, Willie Nelson, Betty White, Cher, Hillary, Taylor Swift and Chevy Chase have all been believed to have died prematurely. We were pretty sure Sylvester Stallone was dead until we saw a bus drive past with *Rambo: Last Blood* plastered across its side. And we all remember when Nelson Mandela died in prison during the 1980s, right? Well, this may not actually be the case (Hoffstad, 2017). The example of a dead city we used at the start of the book, Detroit, has recently shown signs of life and has the potential of becoming a thriving hub of innovation and entrepreneurship.

So, it is possible the whole premise for this book is flawed. We were wrong. Urbanism is not dead. It is just in need of two syringes full of adrenaline to be stabbed into it to bring it back to life.

To paraphrase the immortal Frank Zappa:

Urbanism isn't dead... it just smells funny.

Bibliography

ABS. (1996, June 24). Australian Bureau of Statistics—Special Features: Car use. Retrieved September 28, 2019, from https://www.abs.gov.au/ (catalogue 4102.0)

ABS. (2016). Australian Bureau of Statistics 2016 Census QuickStats: Footscray. Retrieved August 2, 2019, from https://quickstats.censusdata.abs.gov.au/census_services/getproduct/census/2016/quickstat/SSC20929

Agarwal, B. (1997). Re-sounding the alert–gender, resources and community action. World Development, 25(9), 1373–1380.

Agren, D. (2017, January 4). Angry protests erupt across Mexico after 20% hike in gasoline prices. The Guardian. Retrieved from https://www.theguardian.com/world/2017/jan/04/gasolinazo-mexico-gasoline-price-hike-protests-petrol

Alexander, C. (1977). A Pattern Language: Towns, Buildings, Construction. Oxford University Press.

Arida, A. (2002). Quantum City. Abingdon, Oxon: Routledge.

Arnstein, S. R. (1969). A Ladder of Citizen Participation. Journal of the American Institute of Planners, 35(4), 216–224. https://doi.org/10.1080/01944366908977225

Askenaizer, A. (2018). Why are we so nostalgic? – 8-Bit Philosophy. Retrieved September 13, 2019, from https://www.youtube.com/watch?v=DQz8DGEZSQM&t=10s

Atkins, J. (2008). Il Duomo: Brunelleschi, a Man of Many Talents. ADVENTURES IN ARCHITECTURE, 15.

Avanzino, P. (2002). Crimes of the Hot. In Futurama Season 4, Episode 1.

Bacon, E. N. (1974). Design of Cities. Thames and Hudson London.

Barnett, F., Burt, W., & Heath, F. (1944). We must go on—A study of planned reconstruction & housing. Melbourne, Australia.: Wilke & CO. Pty. Ltd.

Batty, M., Besussi, E., & Chin, N. (2003). Traffic, urban growth and suburban sprawl. Centre for Advanced Spatial Analysis, University College London.

Benevolo, L., & Ipsen, C. (1993). The European City. Blackwell Oxford.

Bernstein, F. A. (2005). Seaside at 25: Troubles in Paradise. The New York Times. Retrieved from https://www.nytimes.com/2005/12/09/travel/escapes/seaside-at-25-troubles-in-paradise.html

Berry, L. H., Koski, J., Verkuijl, C., Strambo, C., & Piggot, G. (2019). Making space: How public participation shapes environmental decision-making [Discussion Brief]. Retrieved from Stockholm

Environment Institute website: https://www.sei.org/wp-content/uploads/2019/01/making-space-how-public-participation-shapes-environmental-decision-making.pdf

Berry, S. (2016, June 8). Are we driving ourselves fat? Time spent in car leads to bigger belly. Retrieved October 11, 2019, from The Sydney Morning Herald website: https://www.smh.com.au/lifestyle/health-and-wellness/are-we-driving-ourselves-fat-time-spent-in-car-leads-to-bigger-belly-20160608-gpeqys.html

Bloch, E., & Plaice, N. (1986). The principle of hope (Vol. 3). MIT Press Cambridge, MA.

Bluestone, D. M. (1988). Detroit's City Beautiful and the problem of commerce. Journal of the Society of Architectural Historians, 47(3), 245–262.

Boyd, R. (1968). The Australian Ugliness. Melbourne, Australia: Penguin Books.

Broglio, R. (2008). Technologies of the Picturesque: British art, poetry, and instruments, 1750-1830. New Jersey, US: Associated University Press.

Brown, R. D., & Corry, R. C. (2011). Evidence-based landscape architecture: The maturing of a profession. Landscape and Urban Planning, 100(4), 327–329. https://doi.org/10.1016/j.landurbplan.2011.01.017

Brownson, R. C., Gurney, J. G., & Land, G. H. (1999). Evidence-Based

Decision Making in Public Health: Journal of Public Health Management and Practice, 5(5), 86–97. https://doi.org/10.1097/00124784-199909000-00012

Bruegmann, R. (2006). Sprawl: A compact history. Chicago: University of Chicago press.

Burdette, J.T. (2004). Form-based codes: A cure for the cancer called Euclidean zoning? Virginia Tech, Virginia.

CEA+. (1344). Bodleian Treasures Sappho To Suffrage Marco Polo's Travels—Marco Polo Painting (Marco Polo leaving Venice) [Colour lithograph reproduction]. Retrieved from https://paintingvalley.com/marco-polo-painting#marco-polo-painting-3.jpg

Cerdà, I. (1859). Eixample map of Barcelona. Street section from a "Plan Cerdà" project. Retrieved from https://upload.wikimedia.org/wikipedia/commons/9/9b/Cerda-avantprojecteEixample-1955.jpg

Cerdà, I. (1867). Cerdá: The Five Bases of the General Theory of Urbanization (1999 translation) (A. S. Puig, Ed.; Miller & Fleming, Trans.). Teoría General de la Urbanizaci6n, Electa, Madrid, Spain.: Gingko Pr Inc.

Charting Transport. (2014). Road Traffic | Charting Transport. Retrieved July 18, 2018, from https://chartingtransport.com/category/road-traffic/

CNU. (2015). The Charter of the New Urbanism [Text]. Retrieved July

6, 2019, from CNU website: https://www.cnu.org/who-we-are/charter-new-urbanism

Costello, G., & Rowley, S. (2010). The impact of land supply on housing affordability in the Perth metropolitan region. Pacific Rim Property Research Journal, 16(1), 5–22.

Crabb, A. (2018, August 23). A brief history of seven killings, or how climate policy keeps sinking PMs [Text]. Retrieved September 28, 2019, from ABC News website: https://www.abc.net.au/news/2018-08-23/climate-change-policy-a-brief-history-of-seven-killings/10152616

CSIRO. (2019). Introduction to Climate Futures. Retrieved from Commonwealth Scientific and Industrial Research Organisation website: https://www.climatechangeinaustralia.gov.au/en/climate-projections/climate-futures-tool/introduction-climate-futures/

Daley, J., Coates, B., & Wiltshire, T. (2017). Submission to the NSW Legislative Assembly Committee on Environment and Planning Inquiry into Land Release and Housing Supply in NSW.

Daley, J., Coates, B., Wiltshire, T., & Grattan Institute. (2018). Housing affordability: Re-imagining the Australian Dream (No. 2018–04). Grattan Institute.

Daunton, M. (2004). London's "Great Stink" and Victorian Urban Planning. BBC History.

Davenport, T. (2016). Residents Guide for Objectors | Save Our Suburbs Vic. Assoc. No: A00360675. Retrieved June 27, 2019, from http://sos.asn.au/faqs/residents-guide/

Deffeyes, K. S. (2006). Beyond Oil: The View from Hubbert's Peak. New York: Hill and Wang.

Delatte Jr, N. J. (2009). Beyond Failure: Forensic Case Studies for Civil Engineers. Reston, VA: ASCE Press.

Deterding, S., Dixon, D., Khaled, R., & Nacke, L. (2011). From game design elements to gamefulness: Defining gamification. Proceedings of the 15th International Academic MindTrek Conference: Envisioning Future Media Environments, 9–15. ACM.

Devisch, O., Poplin, A., & Sofronie, S. (2016). The gamification of civic participation: Two experiments in improving the skills of citizens to reflect collectively on spatial issues. Journal of Urban Technology, 23(2), 81–102.

Dodson, J., Sipe, N., & Evans, R. (2008). The VAMPIRE at the Polling Booth: What influence did higher fuel prices and rising mortgage interest rates have at the 2007 Australian Federal Election? Griffith: Griffith University.

Doré, G., & Pannemaker, S. (1872). Over London–by Rail from London: A Pilgrimage [Etching]. Retrieved from https://upload.wikimedia.org/wikipedia/commons/c/c8/Dore_London.jpg

Downs, A. (1962). The law of peak-hour expressway congestion. Traffic

Quarterly, 16(3). Retrieved from https://trid.trb.org/view/694596

Dunne, A., & Raby, F. (2013). Speculative Everything: Design, Fiction, and Social Dreaming. Cambridge, Mass.,: MIT press.

Duty, K., &Tucker, M. (2006). From NIMBY to good neighbors: Recent studies reinforce that apartments are good for a community. National Multi Housing Council, Washington, DC.

DVA. (2016). Planning ahead: A guide to putting your affairs in order. Department of Veterans' Affairs, Australian Government, 56.

Eisenman, P., & Krier, L. (1989). My ideology is better than yours. Architectural Design, London, 2, 6–18.

Ewing, R. H., Pendall, R., & Chen, D. D. (2002). Measuring sprawl and its impact (Vol. 1). Smart Growth America Washington, DC.

Ewing, R., Hamidi, S., Grace, J. B., & Wei, Y. D. (2016). Does urban sprawl hold down upward mobility? Landscape and Urban Planning, 148, 80–88.

Ewing, R., Meakins, G., Hamidi, S., & Nelson, A. C. (2014). Relationship between urban sprawl and physical activity, obesity, and morbidity – Update and refinement. Health & Place, 26, 118–126. https://doi.org/10.1016/j.healthplace.2013.12.008

Extra Credits. (2015). England: The Broad Street Pump - You Know Nothing, John Snow - Extra History - #1. Retrieved from https://www.

youtube.com/watch?v=TLpzHHbFrHY

Fitzpatrick, M., & Dunn, R. (2019). What will climate feel like in 60 years? Retrieved August 9, 2019, from https://fitzlab.shinyapps.io/cityapp/

FNMA. (1997). National Housing Survey, City Life, Homeownership, and the American Dream. Washington, DC: Federal National Mortgage Association (FNMA).

Frank, L. D., Andresen, M. A., & Schmid, T. L. (2004). Obesity relationships with community design, physical activity, and time spent in cars. American Journal of Preventive Medicine, 27(2), 87–96. https://doi.org/10.1016/j.amepre.2004.04.011

Frantz, D. (1999, August 1). The Nation: Disney's Brave New Town; Trouble at the Happiest School on Earth. The New York Times. Retrieved from https://www.nytimes.com/1999/08/01/weekinreview/the-nation-disney-s-brave-new-town-trouble-at-the-happiest-school-on-earth.html

Gallagher, D. (2001). The Modernist Movement: The bubble bursts (1961 - 1979). Retrieved September 22, 2019, from OpenLearn website: https://www.open.edu/openlearn/history-the-arts/history/heritage/the-modernist-movement-the-bubble-bursts-1961-1979

Gilbert, M. (2003). On Beyond Koolhaas Identity, Sameness and the Crisis of City Planning. Umbau 20. Retrieved from https://www.uibk.ac.at/wuv/pdf/ehem/gilbert_city.pdf

Glaeser, E. (2011). Triumph of the City. London: Pan McMillan.

Godwin, M. (1995). Godwin's law of Hitler Analogies (and Corollaries. Retrieved October 23, 2019, from https://web.archive.org/web/20120829094739/http://w2.eff.org/Net_culture/Folklore/Humor/godwins.law

Gordon, P. (2019, April 5). France announces 6% energy price hike – protest expected. Retrieved September 29, 2019, from Smart Energy International website: https://www.smart-energy.com/industry-sectors/business-finance-regulation/france-announces-6-energy-price-hike-further-protests-expected/

Gore, A. (2006, September 11). Interview by Kerry O'Brien. 'Gore in fight for truth on global warming' The 7.30 Report, ABC Television [ABC television program].

Gorzelany, J. (2019). Do you live in the city with the worst traffic? Retrieved October 11, 2019, from Forbes website: https://www.forbes.com/sites/jimgorzelany/2019/02/11/here-are-the-u-s-cities-suffering-the-worst-traffic-congestion/

Griffin, A. (2007, October 12). Contrarian unabashedly bashes Portland, The Monday Profile: Randal O'Toole. The Oregonian. Retrieved from https://web.archive.org/web/20080110121859/http://www.oregonlive.com/news/oregonian/index.ssf?/base/news/119725530930830.xml&coll=7&thispage=1

Hales, L. (2005, October 15). In Mississippi, the Reshape of Things to

Come. Washington Post. Retrieved from https://www.washingtonpost.com/archive/lifestyle/2005/10/15/in-mississippi-the-reshape-of-things-to-come/fa472553-8911-44eb-b408-582c8f2a1c85/

Hansen, J., Johson, D., Lacis, A., Lebedeff, S., Lee, P., & d Rind, R. (1981). Climate impact of increasing atmospheric carbon dioxide. Science, 213, 4511.

Haverfield, F. (1913). Ancient Town-Planning. The Clarendon Press, Oxford UK.

Heanue, S. (2019, January 15). Zimbabwe protests turn deadly after petrol prices become most expensive in the world [Text]. Retrieved September 29, 2019, from ABC News website: https://www.abc.net.au/news/2019-01-15/zimbabwe-protests-turn-deadly-after-fuel-price-hike/10717892

Hoffstad, E. (2017). Internet Comment Etiquette: "Mandela Effect." Retrieved from https://www.youtube.com/watch?v=TYonTBRM0VI

Hutt, R. (2019). These cities have the best quality of life. Retrieved September 6, 2019, from World Economic Forum website: https://www.weforum.org/agenda/2019/05/these-cities-have-the-best-quality-of-life/

IPCC. (2018). Climate Scenario Development. Retrieved from Intergovernmental Panel on Climate Change website: https://www.ipcc.ch/site/assets/uploads/2018/03/TAR-13.pdf

IT, C. C.-R. (2019). Mapping the world's prices 2019. Retrieved September 6, 2019, from Deutsche Bank Research website: https://www.dbresearch.com/PROD/RPS_EN-PROD/PROD0000000000494405/Mapping_the_world%27s_prices_2019.xhtml

Jacobs, A. (1993). Great Streets MIT Press (Vol. 593). Cambridge, MA.

Jacobs, J. (1961). The Death and Life of Great American Cities. New York: Random House.

Jeffries, S. (2015, October 26). 10 things South Park has taught us about gentrification. The Guardian. Retrieved from https://www.theguardian.com/cities/2015/oct/26/what-south-park-teaches-us-about-gentrification

Jencks, C. (2000). Architecture 2000 and Beyond: Success in the Art of Prediction. Michigan: Wiley.

Jupp, J. (2002). From White Australia to Woomera: The Story of Australian Immigration. Cambridge: Cambridge University Press.

Kaplan, M. (1995). Revisiting Fascism: Degenerate art and the new corporate style. Journal of Architecture, 16. (University of Tennessee).

Kelbaugh, D. (2000). Three paradigms: New urbanism, everyday urbanism, post urbanism—An excerpt from the essential common place. Bulletin of Science, Technology & Society, 20(4), 285–289.

Kelly, J.-F., Weidmann, B., & Walsh, M. (2011). The housing we'd choose. Grattan Institute Melbourne.

Kelly-Schwartz, A. C., Stockard, J., Doyle, S., & Schlossberg, M. (2004). Is sprawl unhealthy? A multilevel analysis of the relationship of metropolitan sprawl to the health of individuals. Journal of Planning Education and Research, 24(2), 184–196.

Koolhaas, R., & Mau, B. (1995). Generic Cities. In J. Sigler (Ed.), S,M,L,XL. New York: Monacelli Press.

Kostof, S. (1991). The City Shaped: Urban Patterns and Meanings Through History. London: Thames and Hudson.

Kübler-Ross, E. (1973). On death and dying (1st Edition). London: Routledge.

Kunstler, J. H. (1998). Home from nowhere: Remaking our everyday world for the 21st century. Simon and Schuster.

Langenheim, N., White, M., Barton, J., & Eagleson, S. (2017). Designing with Data for Urban Resilience. International Conference on Computers in Urban Planning and Urban Management, 113–133. Springer.

Laurence, R. (1993). Architects, Planners and the Classical City History Today. History Today, 43.

Le Corbusier. (1929). The City of To-Morrow and Its Planning, 1987 reprint. New York: Payson&Clark Ltd, New York.

Lewis, M. B. (1999). Suburban Backlash: The Battle for the World's Most Liveable City. Melbourne: Bloomings Books.

Li, T., Dodson, J., & Sipe, N. (2018). Examining household relocation pressures from rising transport and housing costs–An Australian case study. Transport Policy, 65, 106–113.

Li, T., Sipe, N., & Dodson, J. (2016). Motor vehicle fleets in oil vulnerable suburbs: A prospect of technology innovations. In Planning After Petroleum (pp. 205–213). Routledge.

Liedstrand, B. (2005). Ten common sense rules for TOD. Retrieved October 9, 2019, from Planetizen—Urban Planning News, Jobs, and Education website: https://www.planetizen.com/node/17471

Litman, T. A. (2019). Generated Traffic and Induced Travel (p. 40). Victoria Transport Policy Institute.

Luhn, A. (2015, June 25). Armenia protests escalate after police turn on demonstrators. The Guardian. Retrieved from https://www.theguardian.com/world/2015/jun/24/armenia-yerevan-protests-electric-prices-russia

Lynch, K. (1981). A Theory of a Good City. Cambridge: MIT Press.

Magrinyà, F., & de Balanzó, R. (2015). Innovación social, innovación urbana y resiliencia desde una perspectiva crítica: El caso de la autoorganización en el espacio urbano de Barcelona. Innovación Social y Políticas Urbanas En España: Experiencias Significativas En Las Grandes Ciudades, 59–94. Icaria.

Malthus, T. R. (1798). An essay on the principle of population (Vol. 1). J. Johnson, London. 1986.

McCann, B. A., & Ewing, R. (2003). Measuring the health effects of sprawl: A national analysis of physical activity, obesity and chronic disease. Retrieved from https://trid.trb.org/view/661006

Mehaffy, M. (2004). A Conversation with Andrés Duany. Katarxis No 3: New Science, New Urbanism, New Architecture?, 3(3).

Merica, D. (2017). Trump dramatically changes US approach to climate change. Retrieved September 28, 2019, from CNN website: https://www.cnn.com/2017/03/27/politics/trump-climate-change-executive-order/index.html

Millado, N., & Vigneri, S. (2012). The fittest and fattest cities in America. Accessed August. Retrieved from http://www.mensfitness.com/traininqllose-weiqhtlthe-fittest-and-fattest-cities-in-america

Moran, A. (2008). How land supply restrictions have locked young people out of the housing market, and how Australia is starting to figure it out. Institute of Public Affairs Review: A Quarterly Review of Politics and Public Affairs, The, 60(3), 54.

Mullin, J. R. (1982). Ideology, Planning Theory and the German City in the Inter-War Years: Part II. Town Planning Review, 53(3), 257.

Mumford, L. (1940). The Culture of Cities (Vol. 19). Secker & Warburg.

NBC. (2018). Police disperse violent protesters in France amid anger over fuel taxes. Retrieved September 29, 2019, from NBC News website: https://www.nbcnews.com/news/world/french-protesters-angry-over-fuel-taxes-clash-police-n939716

Neuman, M. (1998). Does planning need the plan? Journal of the American Planning Association, 64(2), 208–220.

Newig, J. (2007). Does public participation in environmental decisions lead to improved environmental quality?: Towards an analytical framework. Communication, Cooperation, Participation (International Journal of Sustainability Communication), 1(1), 51–71.

Newman, P. (2014). Density, the Sustainability Multiplier: Some Myths and Truths with Application to Perth, Australia. Sustainability, 6(9),

6467–6487. https://doi.org/10.3390/su6096467

Newman, P. G., & Kenworthy, J. R. (1989). Cities and automobile dependence: An international sourcebook. Brookfield, VT: Gower Publishing.

Newton, P. W. (1997). Reshaping cities for a more sustainable future: Exploring the link between urban form, air quality, energy and greenhouse gas emissions. Report of Task Group 6-Urban Infrastructure, to the Australian Academy of Technological Sciences and Engineering for the inquiry into urban air pollution in Australia.

Norman, J. (2016, September 14). "Go back to where you came from": Hanson wants Muslims shut out [Text]. Retrieved October 15, 2019, from ABC News website: https://www.abc.net.au/news/2016-09-14/one-nation-senator-pauline-hanson-makes-first-speech-to-senate/7845150

Pariser, E. (2011). The filter bubble: What the Internet is hiding from you. Penguin UK.

Parker, T. (2015). The City Part of Town. In South Park Series 19. Retrieved from https://southpark.cc.com/full-episodes/s19e03-the-city-part-of-town

PCA. (2015). What is Palliative Care? Retrieved September 22, 2019, from Palliative Care Australia website: https://palliativecare.org.au/what-is-palliative-care

Peirce, N. (2006, December 18). Sustainable Cities. Retrieved October 10, 2019, from The American Prospect website: https://prospect.org/api/content/a5783910-8e04-5f09-9407-40d534437610/

Pollan, M. (1997, December 14). Town-building is no Mickey Mouse operation. The New York Times. Retrieved from https://www.nytimes.com/1997/12/14/magazine/town-building-is-no-mickey-mouse-operation.html

Ramsay, M. A. (2006). John Snow, MD: Anaesthetist to the Queen of England and pioneer epidemiologist. Baylor University Medical Center Proceedings, 19, 24–28. Taylor & Francis.

Realdania. (2007). Copenhagen Agenda for Sustainable Cities. Copenhagen, Denmark.

Recsei, T. (2004, January 2). Recsei, T 2004, 'Planning Our Suburbs—Sound Policies or Fads', Australian Broadcasting Corporation Radio National 576, interview with Tony Recsei by Robyn Williams, 1st February.

Reid, A. (2011). Most Britons support reinstating the death penalty for murder. Retrieved August 15, 2019, from https://web.archive.org/web/20120819163903/http://www.angus-reid.com/wp-content/uploads/2011/08/2011.08.23_Death_BRI.pdf

Rippon, R. (2005). Melbourne: About sustainability and ore. Architect Victoria, (Autumn).

Rose, T., Allom, T., & Pickering, G. (1835). Westmoreland, Cumberland, Durham, and Northumberland, illustrated. Retrieved from https://archive.org/details/westmorelandcumb00rose/page/6

Rowland, K. (1966). The Shape of Towns. Melbourne, Australia: Ginn & Company Ltd.

Sackett, D. L., Rosenberg, W. M. C., Gray, J. A. M., Haynes, R. B., & Richardson, W. S. (1996). Evidence based medicine: What it is and what it isn't. BMJ, 312(7023), 71–72. https://doi.org/10.1136/bmj.312.7023.71

Sandlin, G. (2006). Urbanization & Health University of Washington, Program on the Environment lecture'. Retrieved December 12, 2011, from depts.washington.edu/envir202/Lessons/Lesson05.pdf

Schechtman, S. (2003). How to Live with the NIMBY syndrome the ethical spectacle, Vol. IX, No. 1. Retrieved October 11, 2019, from http://www.spectacle.org/0103/sy.html

Schneider, B. (2018). You can't build your way out of traffic congestion. Or can You? Retrieved September 28, 2019, from CityLab website: https://www.citylab.com/transportation/2018/09/citylab-university-induced-demand/569455/

Schrank, D., & Lomax, T. (2003). The 2003 urban mobility report. Texas Transportation Institute The Texas A&M University System.

Shaw, R. (2018). Generation priced out: Who gets to live in the new urban America. Univ of California Press.

Shilton, T. (2016). Heart Foundation Welcomes Active Policy. Retrieved November 30, 2018, from The Heart Foundation website: https://www.heartfoundation.org.au/news/heart-foundation-welcomes-active-policy

Sitte, C. (1986). City Planning According to Artistic Principles (G. Collins & C. Crasemann Collins, Trans.). New York: Random House.

Sui, D. Z. (2003). Musings on the fat city: Are obesity and urban forms linked? Urban Geography, 24(1), 75–84.

Taylor, M. C. (2001). The Moment of Complexity: Emerging Network Culture. University of Chicago Press.

Teut, A. (1967). Architektur im Dritten Reich (Architecture in the Third Reich), 1933-1945 (Vol. 19). Frankfurt: Ullstein.

Thiel, S.-K., & Fröhlich, P. (2017). Gamification as motivation to engage in location-based public participation? In Progress in Location-Based Services 2016 (pp. 399–421). Springer.

Tolley, R. (2011). Good for Business-The benefits of making streets more walking and cycling friendly. Heart Foundation South Australia.

Tranter, P. (2011). The urban speed paradox: Time pressure, cars and health. Dissent, (36), 9.

Turner, T. (1991). The SAD Design Method vs Pattern Analysis and Design. Retrieved September 23, 2019, from https://www.gardenvisit.com/history_theory/garden_landscape_design_articles/design_methods/sad_design_method

Turner, T., & Watson, D. (2000). Dead masterplans and digital creativity. Presented at the Greenwich, Digital Creativity Symposium, University of Greenwich. Retrieved from https://www.gardenvisit.com/landscape_architecture/computers_design/digital_design_creativity

Tyrwhitt, J. (1947). Patrick Geddes in India; Edited by Jaqueline Tyrwhitt, with an Introd. By Lewis Mumford and a Pref. By HV Lancaster. London, L. Humphries.

Ulm, C. D. (1486). Eunuchus. In H. Neidhart (Trans.), Eunuchus (p. 21). Retrieved from https://www.loc.gov/item/48035772/.

US EPA, O. (2015, December 29). Sources of Greenhouse Gas Emissions [Overviews and Factsheets]. Retrieved September 28, 2019, from US EPA website: https://www.epa.gov/ghgemissions/sources-greenhouse-gas-emissions

Verrone, P. (1999). A Fishful of Dollars [Season 1 Episode 6]. In Futurama, Season 1, Episode 6. Fox Network: Fox Network.

Weiss, A. S. (1995). Mirrors of infinity: The French Formal garden and 17th century metaphysics. Princeton Architectural Press.

White, M. (2007). Densification, Pedestrian Catchments and the Battle for Middle Earth. Can Agent Based Pedestrian Modelling Be Used to Inform Urban Morphology? 51st IFHP 2007 World Congress, Future of Cities - Impacts - Indicators - Implementations. Presented at the Copenhagen. Copenhagen: International Federation for Housing and Planning.

White, M. (2014). Preserving open space amenity using subtractive volumetric modelling. Global Demographic and Climate Challenges in the City, Aachener Geographische Arbeiten, (50), 107–126.

White, M. (2018). Cities of Light [Cities of Light]. Retrieved July 7, 2018, from http://www.marcuswhite.com.au/cities-of-light/

White, M. & Kimm, G. (2015). Measuring sky view factor of urban canyons using hacked Gopro hemispheric video processing. In R. H. Crawford & A. Stephan (Eds.), Research for a Better Built Environment: 49th International Conference of the Architectural Science Association 2015 (pp. 525–535). Retrieved from http://apo.org.au/node/61762

White, M. & Kimm, G. (2018). PedCatch – inclusive pedestrian accessibility modelling using animated service area simulation with crowd sourced network data. In Healthy Future Cities (p. pp.190-202, pp.487–501). Beijing: China Architecture and Building Press.

White, M. & Langenheim, N. (2014). Measuring urban canyons with real-time light based sky view factor modelling. In P.T. Oliveira V Pinho

P, Batista L. & M. C (Eds.), Our common future in Urban Morphology (pp. 239–304). Faculdade de Engenharia da Universidade do Porto.

White, M., & Langenheim, N. (2018). A Spatio-Temporal Decision Support System for Designing with StreetTrees. International Journal of E-Planning Research (IJEPR), 7(4), 1–24.

Wikipedia. (2019). List of Disney live-action remakes of animated films. In Wikipedia. Retrieved from https://en.wikipedia.org/w/index.php?-title=List_of_Disney_live-action_remakes_of_animated_films&ol-did=915426364

Williams, J. A. (2019). When Truckers Shut Down America to Protest Oil Prices—And Became Folk Heroes. Retrieved September 29, 2019, from HISTORY website: https://www.history.com/news/oil-crisis-1973-truck-strike

Witze, A. (2007). That's oil, folks... Nature, 445, 14–17. https://doi.org/10.1038/445014a

Note: This book draws upon initial concepts and text from Marcus' PhD thesis 'Informing an Integrated and Sustainable Urbanism through Rapid, Defragmented Analysis and Design' (2009) at RMIT University Melbourne in the Spatial Information Architecture Laboratory.

THE PRACTICE OF THEORY AND THE THEORY OF PRACTICE

The Deutsche Nationalbibliothek lists this publication in the Deutsche Nationalbibliografie; detailed bibliographic information is available on the internet at http://dnb.d-nb.de

The Death of Urbanism -Transitions Through Five Stages of Grief
Marcus White and Nano Langenheim

ISBN: 978-3-88778-563-5
Publication © by Spurbuchverlag 1. print run 2019
Am Eichenhügel 4, 96148 Baunach, Germany

AADR – Art Architecture Design Research publishes research with an emphasis on the relationship between critical theory and creative practice.
AADR Curatorial Editor: Prof Dr Rochus Urban Hinkel, Stockholm
Production: pth-mediaberatung GmbH, Würzburg
Graphic Design: Moa Sundkvist, Stockholm